Maritime America

Art and Artifacts
from America's
Great Nautical Collections

Edited and Introduced by
Peter Neill

Balsam Press, Inc. *in affiliation with* Harry N. Abrams, Inc., New York

ACKNOWLEDGMENTS

Any successful maritime enterprise needs the participation of a committed and talented crew. The editor wishes to express grateful appreciation to all the contributors for their confidence in and support of the project; to Jean Hoots and Melissa Pierson for their close reading of the copy; to Harriet Ripinsky for her production counsel and supervision; to Greer Allen for his inspired design; to Robert Morton of Harry N. Abrams, Inc., for his willingness to take this book twice; and to Barbara Krohn of Balsam Press for her willingness to take it on once and for all, and then to work with such determination, enthusiasm, and skill on its behalf.

—*Peter Neill*

Library of Congress Cataloging in Publication Data
Main entry under title:
Maritime america: art and artifacts from america's great nautical collections
     Includes index.
     1. Marine art. 2. Maritime.   I. Neill, Peter, 1941–
N8230.M4 1988   704.9'437'074013—dc19   88-1386
ISBN 0-8109-1527-8
ISBN 0-917439-11-2

Published by Balsam Press, Inc.
122 East Twenty-fifth Street, New York, N.Y., 10010
in affiliation with Harry N. Abrams, Inc., New York
A Times Mirror Company
Manufactured in Hong Kong by Mandarin Offset
Designed by Greer Allen
Edited by Barbara Krohn

Frontispiece: *The restored 1877 barque* Elissa *under sail off Galveston Island*

Title page: *Detail of a colored lithograph showing a view of Boston Harbor in 1848*

Opposite: *Lapstrake construction, one of the technical contributions of the Vikings, is practiced and taught, as it was for a thousand years, at the Rockport Apprenticeshop.*

Contents

Introduction

Peter Neill, President,
The South Street Seaport Museum,
New York

A Nation Built by Water

The "new" world was discovered by hardy foreigners in boats—whether Norse, Italian, or Spanish, it does not much matter. In a splendid proof of human ingenuity, they navigated unknown ocean to find a continent defensively shored, with protected harbors and estuaries, and a native population supported by abundant marine life. As their successors explored, they defined vast areas, north to south, east to west, by water. Their villages and towns lined bays and banks; their cities were founded at the confluence of rivers. Their transportation and communication were water-borne. Their energy was water-driven. Their food was water-grown. America was a water-land, and its character, organization, and institutions were thereby created.

The accounts that you will read in the ensuing pages are persuasive. New York, Philadelphia, and Boston were cities that emerged as great ports, centers for transoceanic commerce wherein grew such related enterprise as banking, insurance, and central markets. Other cities and towns were elements of coastal and internal trade, depots or transfer points for lumber, ore, furs, cotton, tobacco, sugar, and other agricultural products. Nantucket and Mystic were whaling centers. Bath, Salem, and Norfolk were shipbuilding towns. Their character and complexity were determined by this maritime activity: physical plan and architecture, political organization, class divisions, family fortunes and misfortunes—the social history of young America.

This book attempts to document this rich panorama through the collections of several of our nation's finest maritime museums. Thirteen organizations are represented here; the Council of American Maritime Museums has thirty-four members, and hundreds of other museums, libraries, and historical societies possess important maritime materials. Much of this heritage also remains in private hands, in the collections of individuals and in the ownership of thousands of classic vessels still in use. Wherever there is water, our maritime patrimony can still be found.

The contents that follow are arranged as a voyage, a chronological journey that

4
The Maine coast

descends the east coast of the United States, jumps westward, and then returns. I urge you to view each chapter as a port of call, as a place to be savored as though you were transported from your armchair, as an experience to be understood with all the faculties of a sophisticated traveler.

The earliest sophisticated travelers, of course, were seamen themselves who accumulated the "natural and artificial curiosities such as are to be found beyond the Cape of Good Hope and Cape Horn." The results of these explorations and expeditions were the founding elements of the magnificent collections of our oldest maritime museum, the Peabody Museum of Salem. Ethnographic materials, paintings, China Trade artifacts, ocean liner memorabilia, logbooks and maritime journals are among the other strengths of the museum's exemplary holdings as described by Director Peter J. Fetchko and Curator Paul Forsythe Johnston. The Peabody is the originator of many excellent exhibits and catalogs and is the home of *The American Neptune,* our most important scholarly publication on maritime history.

As the first immigrants were Europeans, it seems fitting that we continue with the magnificent *Nederlandische* whaling scenes of the Kendall Whaling Museum in Sharon, Massachusetts, as described by Director Stuart M. Frank. Indeed, artistic heritage, like commercial heritage, had its precursors on the Continent, but, at the same time, whaling was one of America's first "industries," and our flag flew competitively among the ships of the international fleet on distant whaling grounds. The Kendall is the finest of many small museums devoted to whaling, and maintains a fascinating collection of whaling documents, art, implements, and scrimshaw.

The collections of the Mystic Seaport Museum are equally distinguished—paintings, prints, drawings, photographs of classic yachts, and figureheads are among the most significant outlined by Associate Editor Andrew W. German. But Mystic's collections transcend those of traditional museums to include ships, a marvelous assemblage of small craft in and out of water, and numerous authentic buildings and artifacts associated with the trades typical of a New England shoreline village. In the meticulous and accurate restoration of its holdings, Mystic has set the standard for us all. It is a major tourist attraction with the highest visitation of any maritime museum in the United States, if not the world.

At South Street, ships and buildings are also a primary focus. In Chapter Four, the emergence of New York as the nation's preeminent port is narrated. Waves of immigrants passed through "the street of ships": the goods, people, and ideas that created major commercial and cultural institutions that remain powerful elements in American economic and social life today. Our historic fleet is the largest in tonnage anywhere and is an extraordinary resource and challenge to maintain and restore.

Our journey then continues north to the St. Lawrence River, where Laurie Watson

Rush and Dawn E. Rusho describe the Thousand Islands Shipyard Museum and its collection of small craft, sleek runabouts, outboard engines, and memorabilia of island life. Here was the location of the early Gold Cup and hydroplane races prior to World War I and of adventuresome rumrunning during Prohibition.

During the colonial era, Philadelphia was a port comparable in vigor to the City of London. Museum Historian Philip Chadwick Foster Smith of the Philadelphia Maritime Museum narrates the city's history as reflected in its collections and growing schedule of exhibits. Philadelphia, of course, is still a major port, and the museum is emerging as an energetic and imaginative presence in that city's cultural life.

The Calvert Marine Museum in Solomons, Maryland, is described by its director, Ralph Eshelman. One of several fine museums devoted to the distinctive maritime traditions of the Chesapeake Bay, Calvert documents the life of local watermen, the oyster fishery from harvest to market, and the history of the Patuxent River, site of important naval engagements during the War of 1812.

Newport News, Virginia, is the home of the Mariners' Museum and its extraordinary collections of ship models, regional small craft, and marine pictures. Recently, the museum was selected by the National Oceanic and Atmospheric Administration to be the primary repository of artifacts related to the Civil War ironclad *Monitor,* which fought to its historic draw with the *Merrimac* in nearby Hampton Roads. Of all our maritime museums, Mariners'—as Associate Curator Richard C. Malley's chapter will reveal—is certainly the most eclectic and international in scope.

The exhibits of the North Carolina Maritime Museum in Beaufort, North Carolina, reveal the direct relationship of maritime history and marine science. Curator Michael B. Alford evokes the storm-battered coastline, barrier islands, and estuaries that determined the shape and content of the region's fishing culture and its varied watercraft and local custom.

From thence we move westward, following the course of settlers to the freshwater lakes and rivers of the nation. The Manitowoc Maritime Museum in Manitowoc, Wisconsin, is one of several throughout the Great Lakes region whose collections document the history of lakes shipping and transportation. Director Burt Logan presides over a young and aggressive museum and delivers a narrative not familiar enough to those of us back east in provincial New England.

The Mississippi is one of the great waterways of the world, the spine of a river system incorporating the Ohio, the Missouri, and myriad others, extending maritime culture into every levee town and backwater along the way. These rivers crossed America's heartland, and their traditions are uniquely ours. Director Jerome Enzler and Curator Roger R. Osborne describe the collections of the Woodward Riverboat Museum in Dubuque, Iowa, which represent the colorful history of the steamboat era.

Finally, we address the preservation of maritime skills. The restoration of the barque *Elissa* is one of our great successes, the transformation of a derelict sailing ship into an operable vessel capable of making the passage from Galveston, Texas, to New York City for Operation Sail 1986 and the Statue of Liberty centennial celebration. Peter H. Brink, Executive Director of the Galveston Historical Foundation, describes the remarkable collaboration of craftsmen and volunteers who came together from all over the United States to make *Elissa* possible.

The perpetuation of maritime skills is also the purpose of the Rockport Apprenticeshop, Rockport, Maine, one of a growing number of boat-building programs across the nation. Director Lance R. Lee is a passionate advocate of youth training, international exchange, and the survival of values associated with maritime craft and on-the-water experience. While not a formal "museum," the 'Shop is very much a collection—of small boat history and construction detail, of anthropological information from all maritime nations, and of talented and committed individuals.

Each chapter, of course, is interesting in its own right, but they also offer revealing contrasts. Compare, for example, the Kendall Whaling Museum and the Rockport Apprenticeshop: both are New England–oriented, both directors quote Melville, both avidly collect, both publish, both reflect the influence of international maritime culture on our own. And yet, these two organizations are almost antithetical in their public personae and in the audiences they serve.

Other possible comparisons include the collecting policies of the Peabody, Mystic, Mariners', and Kendall; or the interpretative approaches of Philadelphia and South Street, two urban museums, with those of North Carolina and Manitowoc, two regional museums. Contrast attitudes toward the keeping of ships and boats: the large fleets at South Street and Mystic with the single vessels at Galveston and Dubuque; contrast keeping these large fleets with the small craft collections at Mystic, Mariners', Calvert, and Thousand Islands. Contrast attitudes toward the keeping of buildings: the restoration of existing on-site structures at South Street, Galveston, and Calvert with the off-site collecting of authentic structures brought together in an "exemplary maritime village" at Mystic. Compare salt water, fresh water, and brackish places in between; compare how each institution presents itself as a unique keeper of nautical heritage, as an interpreter and celebrant of the past.

Connections

"The sea connects all things." I first read this simple statement in an article by historian Gaddis Smith and I can recall my foolish sense of revelation at the truth of the assertion. Here was both the fact and metaphor whereby to express the essence of our maritime history: the physical and psychological connection from past to future. Having

5
"USS Constitution *Escaping From the British, July, 1812" by Julian O. Davidson. "Old Ironsides," her keel laid in 1794, remains an active vessel in the U.S. Navy. This painting is part of the exhibition at the USS* Constitution *Museum, located adjacent to the ship in the Charlestown Navy Yard, Boston, Massachusetts.*

5

asked you to compare and contrast, I invite you now to connect—to connect with the overwhelming influence of things maritime on the history of the United States, with the diversity and vitality of the various organizations that are the custodians of our invaluable marine artifacts and skills, with a tradition that remains, indeed grows, today.

In our time, history seems almost detached from our present and our purpose. We live in an era labeled "the information age" when all things are documented, not discovered. Ironically, this surfeit of data appears to have denied, certainly devalued, our efforts to understand the past. To combat this sad state of affairs, historians frequently organize their information into a system of themes and turning points—into instructive connections and moments of disconnection. One such pervasive theme in these pages is fishing, a formative aspect of maritime culture along all three coasts. From Maine to the Carolinas, from the Keys to Galveston Bay, from Mexico to Puget Sound, marine food production provided occupation for many and sustenance for all. And each species— whether lobster, oyster, sardine, cod, shrimp, crab, salmon, or what have you— demanded its individualized technology (boat type, knots, nets, pots, weirs) and individualized knowledge (migration history, spawning pattern, weather signs, specialized seamanship). Around each fishery grew an identifiable culture (craftsmanship, storytelling, ritual) that was passed on through the generations to become part of a unique local narrative and sense of place. This tradition—this connection—is both cause and effect of history.

An alternative method to the same end is to examine the disconnections, the significant points of diversion or sudden change that, too, partake of cause and effect. One such is the nineteenth-century invention of the steam engine with its enormous impact on the design and operation of ships. Trans-Atlantic passage, for example, became a matter of days instead of months. Steamboats triumphed over the upstream passage; steamers made overnight excursions from New York to Boston and Albany. The ports enlarged their capacity through the efforts of steam-powered tugs, derricks, and ferryboats. And, of course, as steam brought the end of the age of sail, it empowered the railroad.

What a time for enterprise! Ship owners suddenly became railroad builders. New areas of the country were opened, new products delivered more speedily and directly to market. It was as if a second national network of transport was overlaid on the waterways, a competitive alternative that was ultimately to render canal and river carriers inefficient and uneconomical for all but a few bulk cargoes. Steam had an enormous impact on maritime communities. Shipyards were forced to convert from wood construction to iron, then steel; from carpentry to riveting to welding. Many companies could not make the transition and populations overly dependent on this specific trade felt the terrible effect. Many workers could not, or would not, be retrained. New techniques required fewer man-hours with inevitable layoffs; employers were less paternalistic; working conditions became more difficult and dangerous. It is not surprising to learn that early labor organization took place in the maritime trades where, as the physical scale got larger, the human scale declined, and the workforce could find protection and advocacy only in unionism.

Thus, a single technological change advanced widespread social change. Similar events in more recent history such as the pipeline or the airplane have in turn taken another segment of maritime business by moving more product quicker at less cost to more destinations. The container ship is a contemporary example, a post–World War II advance in ship design that completely disrupted prior scale with the necessary construction of deeper draft ports in new locations, more automated cargo handling facilities, new regulatory authority, the accelerated obsolescence of the existing merchant fleet—all this even further reducing employment. The resultant physical relocation costs and contract settlements are measurable; the costs to the communities in which these changes took place are not so easily determined. Put all this in the context of national recessions and vigorous international competition and you will discover a decline in American maritime enterprise so severe that recovery is questionable.

Maritime America Today

The pessimists have a good case. The condition of American waterfronts is appalling. Barriers of railroad lines, superhighways, and dilapidated piers separate most urban populations from the water. That marvelous aggregation of ships and boats of all shapes and sizes tied along New York's South Street simply disintegrated—until the late 1960s when ship preservationists there began desperately to collect what could be found remaining. The vessels of South Street, like those of Mystic Seaport and the San Francisco Maritime Museum, were found derelict and abandoned in international backwaters, their dignity salvageable only through long and loving restoration. A recent survey enumerated fewer than 250 large vessels of historic value in the United States, and the great majority of these are warships built during World War II. In reality, the physical evidence of a glorious aspect of American life has all but disappeared.

What is even more disturbing is the apparent indifference to the situation by the various public and private institutions that traditionally care about such things. Following Operation Sail 1976, the wonderful reunion of tall ships in New York Harbor in celebration of our bicentennial, national awareness of things maritime was renewed. Thereafter, Congress appropriated $5 million for a one-time investment in the preservation of our maritime heritage, principally in the form of ships around the nation in various stages of deterioration. That's it, all of it, ever. Compare that, for example, with the hundreds of millions allocated for preservation of historic landside structures or with the additional tax incentives for private investors in these same buildings. Compare that with the *annual* contribution to the arts by the smallest state in the nation. Compare that with the construction cost of a single tank. I can think of no aspect of our history that has received less from the cultural support apparatus; frankly, it's a national embarrassment.

Why? It is difficult to understand when you examine the comprehensiveness and quality of what graces the following pages. Have the ships lost their magic? No, not true. Have the custodians been too insular, too regional in scope? Yes, true in part. Has our potential constituency diminished? No, not true. Have our organizations been unable or unwilling to *advocate* the value of the patrimony held, to demonstrate with energy and sophistication our need? Yes, too true, indeed. Despite the efforts of earnest individuals and some organizations, no national leadership for the maritime preservation movement has emerged; without it, these archives, these fine arts, these artifacts, these ships may remain best-kept secrets.

This despair extends directly to the marine trades. Shipyards continue to fail throughout the United States. Most of those surviving, such as Bath Iron Works and Newport News, do so on military contracts. New York City, once a great shipbuilding center, is down to two yards, subsisting primarily on repairs. In the 1970s, the American shipbuilding industry could not protect itself against foreign competition, particularly from Japan and Korea, where labor costs and government subsidies made their prices irresistible.

The problem also extends to fisheries, troubled nationwide by high operating and insurance costs, low prices at the dock (but high prices in the market), cutthroat competition from foreign ships on U.S. grounds, and tons of frozen product trucked down from Canada or up from Mexico. Fishermen, typically an independent lot, have organized cooperatives, fought real estate developers for pier space, lobbied for tax incentives, and opened their own retail outlets to maintain profits. It is a tough battle, and, while per capita consumption of fish is increasing, the fishing industry remains troubled. Government support has been erratic and frequently ineffectual. The number of boats allegedly "lost" has become a critical problem for insurance companies; the number of defaults on fishing-boat construction and purchase loans is up; the number of sons following fathers to sea is down.

Maritime America Tomorrow

Optimists do exist, and I number myself among them. It has become clear to me that while it is unreasonable to expect that maritime culture can ever return to its nineteenth-century dimension or splendor, a variety of changes and shakeouts, many already underway, suggest a possible renewal. Let me review some hopeful signs.

First, our waterfronts are being rediscovered, and there is hardly a city with a harbor or a levee that does not have waterside development built or proposed. These

6
Inshore commercial fishing remains a colorful, albeit diminished, part of American maritime life. The Maine Maritime Museum, Bath, Maine, devotes much of its collection and program to this tradition, focusing particularly on the techniques and customs of lobster and sardine fisheries.

projects tend to retail, office, or residential use, high return programs to compensate for the admittedly higher costs of building in a marine environment. The Federal Coastal Zone Management Act has caused many states and cities to prepare plans that protect, in fact encourage, such less profitable, water-related uses as beaches, marshes, and other recreational areas, marinas, port facilities, fishing fleets, and shipyards. A plan is no panacea, and market forces will too often prevail. But there is a suggestion of a new awareness on the part of city officials of the need for public access to the water and support for marine business.

Happily, the public is demanding change. The abandoned piers of New York City have become *de facto* parks with sunbathers and picnickers finding their way through the broken piles and rotten stringers to claim a place apart from the exigencies of urban living. The people of Portland, Maine, have voted overwhelmingly by referendum to maintain their "working waterfront." California has attempted to legislate a public accessway the entire length of its magnificent coastline, a typically controversial land use approach that has drawn much attention in the courts.

The explosion of recreational boaters has also been important. Public ramps for trailered boats have become a major budget item on state agendas. Marina slips are in such demand that cooperative and condominium schemes (at sometimes precipitous prices) have become widespread and some towns have sought statutory protection for some percentage of rentals. Entrepreneurs have begun to see marina development as profitable; many smaller marinas have been purchased by large management companies, bringing greater efficiency to their operation. Membership in yacht clubs, old and new, has flourished. At South Street, we have founded the Manhattan Yacht Club, a unique time-sharing scheme for racing and recreational yachtsmen that prorates the cost of boat ownership, dockage, and maintenance among users. Sailors leave their Wall Street offices, change their clothes, and step aboard a J-24 rigged and ready, just minutes away.

Water-borne recreation today takes many forms. Rowing, for example, long the domain of the college crew, or canoeing and kayaking and white-water rafting; these activities are not only accessible and physically and psychologically rewarding to large numbers of participants, but are also profitable to those businesses that serve them. There are classic runabout shows and Gold Cup reunions in Washington, Nevada, and New York; ice-boating in Minnesota; classic yacht parades and small craft exhibits in Maine, Rhode Island, and Connecticut; Everglades air boating and cruising in Louisiana swamp buggies, fishing derbies, log-canoe and schooner races, catboat rendezvous, friendship weekends, and Hobie Cats on the highways en route to one regatta after another. On-the-water recreation is as elitist as the Southern Ocean Racing Circuit and as populist as the ubiquitous Windsurfer on the cartop of everyman.

A comparable change is seen in the excursion business. Ten years ago, New York

City had the Circle Line and *Pioneer,* South Street's one-hundred-year-old schooner, to take passengers. Today, the harbor is crowded with dinner boats and yachts, excursion vessels and charters. The Maine Windjammers, a wonderful fleet of traditional schooners Down East, now advertise successfully in the national media to recruit passengers for week-long sailing cruises in Penobscot Bay. New coastal cruise ships have also emerged, well appointed and reasonably priced, with itineraries that include Nantucket, Martha's Vineyard, Mystic, the Connecticut River, and the small harbors of Chesapeake Bay. The *Delta Queen* and other riverboats negotiate the snags and tricky shallows of the Mississippi and Ohio. Canal-boat tours are planned, reclaiming the New York State canal system as a recreational resource. Cruising sailboat and trawler yachts extend their range to the extraordinary and generally unfamiliar waters of Nova Scotia or the San Juan Islands.

And for the most inexpensive excursions yet offered, ride the Washington State ferries or, cheaper yet, New York's Staten Island Ferry, twenty-five cents, one way—Statue of Liberty view and return trip no charge.

A concurrent resurgence in the marine trades can also be seen. All these boats and related equipment must be manufactured, distributed, and sold, either in retail outlets or by catalogue. Marine electronics have experienced a particularly profitable recent expansion. Although boat design and manufacture remain difficult business at best, several new designs and classes have emerged as commercial successes. Specialty boat yards such as the North End Yard in Maine, Cutt and Case in Maryland, or Dutch Wharf in Connecticut provide winter storage, repair, and restoration to windjammers and other classic wooden vessels. New excursion-boat construction has breathed life back into certain medium-sized yards in Florida. A surfeit of Gulf off-shore crew boats was suddenly relocated eastward to be converted into private ferries connecting New Jersey to Manhattan Island. These phenomena require skilled labor, and one can speculate that they represent intimations of a more healthy future for the marine trades.

Where will these workers come from? Some will be those who have found personal satisfaction in pursuing a craft. Many will be practiced carpenters, having been converted from the building trades to the more refined challenges of the shipwright's practice. Others will come from more traditional sources such as mechanics' and metalworkers' training schools. Still others will come from marine engineering programs such as Maine Maritime and the Merchant Marine Academy, King's Point, New York. Still others will find placement based on experience gained from service in the Navy or Coast Guard. It is almost as if the marine trades are passing through a generational time warp, shaking out, preparing to abandon despair and to emerge on the other side into a realm of possibility.

I wonder if the same thing might be true for fishing. Several factors apply beyond the cooperative organizing seen in Gloucester, New Bedford, Stonington, Fernadina

7

Beach, Galveston, San Francisco, and Seattle. Clearly, the American diet has changed and the popularity of fish has increased dramatically. Fish, veal, and pasta now dominate menus previously mostly beef. The consumer has also become more sophisticated, with product like tuna steak or monkfish or squid, heretofore largely ignored, becoming profitable. Fish is also being sold differently and more aggressively—in supermarkets, for example, traditionally an outlet for frozen product only, or in retail shops that make a fetish of freshness. Fish "seasons" are anticipated, such as the availability of shad, shad roe, or soft-shell crabs, and at least one restaurant in New York will cook your filet to order—done, that is, just cooked through, or underdone, pink like that perfect steak of yesteryear.

Over the last decade there has been much talk of aquaculture as well. Trout farms, abalone fields, catfish ranches, mussel factories. Bright ideas, big money. I take more solace in the determined profit motive of quahog diggers on Cape Cod or scallopers in Niantic or clammers in Great South Bay or natural growth oystermen in Norwalk. I put more faith in the draggers from New Bedford or the skipjack captains from Tilghman Island or the shrimpers from Corpus Christi or the trawlers from Astoria. Some day, aquaculture may displace fishing; it will do so that much more quickly if environmental degradation of fish habitats continues at its present rate. For almost two decades, biologists have warned of the negative impact of sewage, groundwater run-off, and chemical disposal into our waters. Red tides and PCB counts have become a familiar part of the lexicon. The taking of shellfish is prohibited along much of the Connecticut shoreline.

7
Clearwater, *a replica of a Hudson River sloop, sails the length of the river teaching marine science and promoting public awareness of environmental issues.*

8
In almost every harbor of the United States, condominium development threatens traditional water-related activity. In Maine and California, citizens have voted to restrict development that would destroy working piers, shipyards, marinas, lighthouses, and coastal recreational and natural areas.

Striped bass are no longer available for sale or consumption. The causes of these various effects have been identified, the scholarly articles written, the solutions proposed, and yet, good intentions and political rhetoric aside, progress is negligible.

These varied manifestations of renewed interest in maritime endeavors are diffuse, distributed widely about the country and driven not so much by central policy but rather by localized interest and grass-roots logic. One way to judge the shape and size of this change is to look at the birth and expansion of publications that serve the constituencies. Surely the best example is *Wooden Boat* magazine, founded ten years ago by Jon Wilson, a young man keeping warm in the Maine woods with a bright idea. *Wooden Boat* now has a circulation of over 100,000 and is filled with editorial matter deemed essential by all those concerned with the technology of wooden boat building and maintenance. It is also fat with advertising—for builders of all varieties of vessels, for marine products, tools, and fastenings, for used boats, and for boat-building schools across the nation. Did *Wooden Boat* create this audience, or was it already there? Both, of course; existing interest was unified by the magazine, the magazine fired additional interest, and Jon and his colleagues get deserved credit for a "renaissance."

Wooden Boat is not alone. *Nautical Quarterly* is an elegant sister publication, devoted more to the aesthetics of vessels than to details of their construction. *Sea History*, published by the National Maritime Historical Society, serves the maritime historian and ship preservationist; *Small Boat Journal* serves the small boat enthusiast; *Soundings*, a newspaper appearing in six editions nationally, serves everyone interested in regional maritime activity; *National Fisherman*, another in newspaper format, serves the fishing industry; *Seaport*, published by the South Street Seaport Museum, serves those interested in the maritime history of New York and the nation.

There are many, many more such publications for yachtsmen, powerboaters, antique-boat collectors, fishermen, SCUBA divers. The point is that their success is found in the consolidation of a special maritime interest. Collectively, they define an enormous national audience; together, they reveal the full dimension of maritime America.

More Connections

Those readers familiar with the maritime museums of the United States will note conspicuous omissions in the following pages. Because of the cooperative financial requirements of this project, some very fine museums with exemplary collections could not participate. Among them are the Maine Maritime Museum, Bath, Maine; the Chesapeake Bay Maritime Museum, St. Michael's, Maryland; and the National Maritime Museum, San Francisco, a unit of the National Park Service. The absence of the latter, along with that of museums in San Diego, California, and Astoria, Oregon, means that we can do little to celebrate the extraordinary maritime history of the Pacific Rim. Similarly, the Canadian museums could not join us, and so the special maritime cultures of Nova Scotia, the Canadian Great Lakes, and the Pacific coast are not included. This is regrettable, and the only solace I can offer is that these institutions, and the others listed in the appendix, remain to be explored. These are connections still to be made.

You will also find very little mention here of naval history, a major aspect of American maritime history to be sure. The USS Constitution Museum, Boston, Massachusetts, the USS *Intrepid* Museum, New York, New York, and the U.S. Naval History Museum and Smithsonian Institution, Washington, D.C., are among the foremost collections of such material in the United States. This decision, again determined in part by financial constraints, also reflects the existence of several comparable pictorial volumes devoted to naval history. Numerous other organizations exist, typically focused on a specific naval engagement, such as the U.S. Navy Memorial, Pearl Harbor, or the career of a single warship, such as the battleship *Massachusetts*, Fall River, Massachusetts; the nuclear submarine *Nautilus*, Groton, Connecticut; the battleship *Texas*, Corpus Christi, Texas; and the liberty ship *Jeremiah O'Brien*, San Francisco, California. These, too, are listed in the appendix.

Nor have we touched on landside structures (other than those associated with the participants). Lighthouses and life-saving stations are an integral part of our maritime culture and their conservation is an extremely popular undertaking with preservationists everywhere. There are numerous other such structures, of course: piers and levees, countinghouses and warehouses, locks and lockhouses, dams, ropewalks, foundries, shipyards, boat shops, and chandleries. The houseboat communities of Sausilito, California, and Lake Union, Washington, are a further example. Many of these buildings are being saved through preservation incentives and adaptive reuse, conversion to restaurants, bed-and-breakfasts, studios, offices, and residences. It is clear that their value has been recognized even if they have not all been converted to museums.

Replicas are another omission, because so many of them are failures. Most of these projects have been the result of civic enthusiasm for the celebration of an historic anniversary. Typically, they have been poorly researched, badly built, and ill-conceived for life after the event has passed and the original enthusiasm waned. There are hulks of replicas built for such occasions within the last ten years. Of course, there are also exceptions, most notably the *Mayflower* in Plymouth, Massachusetts, the *Godspeed* in Virginia, and the *Clearwater*, a Hudson River sloop in New York. Here, too, all three ships required major reconstruction shortly after building. What sets them apart, however, is a financial support system based on public visitation or an innovative environmental education program that generates the funds adequate for their annual operation and maintenance. Undoubtedly, as more and more original vessels are lost, more and more replicas will be built. And new enthusiasms will abound. Funding is being avidly sought today, for example, for three different sets of *Santa Maria*, *Niña*, and *Pinta* ships to grace the Columbus Quincentennial Jubilee in various locales in 1992.

A far more progressive use for replicas and/or newly constructed ships is found in on-the-water educational programs. Of these, the Sea Education Association of Woods Hole, Massachusetts, stands out. SEA operates *Westward* on an ambitious itinerary in Canadian and Caribbean waters. Students from numerous universities enroll in an accredited curriculum in marine science and oceanography. Unlike sail-training programs, in which operating the vessel is the primary activity, SEA views sailing the ship as a necessary adjunct to the more important task of study and research. Two aspects here are important: first, the program's *content*, which goes beyond some romantic notion of living before the mast, and second, the tuition that is paid to meet the ship's demanding budget. SEA is building a second boat, the *Corwith Cramer*, a refinement of *Westward*, and will ultimately operate both in two oceans.

Another variation on this approach is found in the Sound School, a program of the Board of Education of New Haven, Connecticut. The school offers inner-city students a full high school curriculum taught in a marine environment. History is maritime history; English is literature of the sea and writing in personal logbooks; mathematics is basic skills required for navigation and weekly work in the small boat shop; science is marine biology; athletics is sailing in New Haven harbor in sixteen-foot sharpies built by the school. The program is run in conjunction with the Connecticut State University system and Schooner, Inc., a private nonprofit educational organization that operates the sailing research vessel, *J.N. Carter*. Classes are taught aboard the *Carter* and in a waterside facility presently under construction to incorporate traditional classrooms with laboratories, an expanded boat-building facility, and a marine railroad.

The Sound School is part of a growing movement to preserve maritime skills. The assumption is that such an education transcends simple vocational purpose by creating an atmosphere in which to "connect" through teaching and learning. Some members of the school's four graduating classes have enlisted in the Coast Guard and others have found employment in the marine trades; but most have simply benefited from an uncommon alternative to the norm, a substantive educational experience named by the Ford Foundation in 1986 as one of the "twenty most innovative public programs in America."

Nautical Archaeology

With the advent of SCUBA, magnetometry, side-scan sonar, and other underwater technologies, numerous manifestations of maritime America, heretofore lost, became accessible. Ships and machinery, cargo and equipment, all apparently lost to the historical record, are now recoverable—a potential that has caused much excitement and consternation among maritime historians, archaeologists, and preservationists.

9
Following its famous encounter with the Merrimac, *the Civil War ironclad* Monitor *was wrecked in 200 feet of water off Cape Hatteras, North Carolina. The ship is being protected and studied by the National Oceanic and Atmospheric Administration, a federal agency. This computer-generated perspective rendering of the ship, lying inverted on its "cheesebox" turret, was developed from three-dimensional sonar data collected by a remotely operated research vehicle directed by the Woods Hole Oceanographic Institute and the U.S. Navy during a June 1987 expedition to the wreck site.*

9

Several discoveries illustrate the situation.

The most controversial has been the *Atocha* Project, a seventeenth-century Spanish ship found by salvor Mel Fischer in waters off Florida after a long, compulsive search financed by hundreds of small investors. Fischer's perseverance—or luck—paid off, for the *Atocha* and her sister ship were carrying literally millions of dollars in Spanish gold. These artifacts were subsequently recovered in a manner that has met with criticism, indeed condemnation, by professional archaeologists who view the undertaking as "treasure hunting" indifferent to the more disciplined practices of their science.

Laws of salvage, established long before underwater exploration was even imagined, permit this kind of recovery without constraint. The salvor is, in fact, motivated by the salvage value of what he seeks, not by its aesthetic importance or its contribution to scholarship and our understanding of history. This is not the case, of course, landside. There, should such a discovery be made, federal and state law, legislated as a result of landside abuse, protects the find from commercial exploitation and enforces standards of archaeological investigation. Several years ago, a developer, excavating an office tower site in lower Manhattan, came upon the remains of a ship. The city had been expanded throughout its history by successive landfills, and frequently old piers, their abandoned ships tied to, were simply buried to create new real estate. Imagine the amazement, then, as the bulldozers uncovered those old bones; imagine also the delay and expense to the developer who, by law, was required to finance a serious archaeological dig which eventually removed and conserved the ship and its related materials in a museum. Such instances are becoming more and more frequent, and most construction projects landside today require comparable protection and inquiry. A serious attempt is being made to pass appropriate federal legislation to extend this requirement to endangered cultural resources underwater.

A second example is seen in the discovery of the *Titanic*, assumed to have been lost forever. Here, public interest is at its highest, and yet the discoverers proposed—and the American public agreed—that the ship should remain undisturbed beyond photographic documentation, indeed, even that its location be kept as secret as possible. But as I write, a French expedition is exploring the wreck and recovering artifacts with a robot submersible more than two miles below the ocean surface. Motivated by the possibility of extraordinary monetary gain, and assisted by such technology, salvors may overcome all obstacles, including public opinion.

A third example is the USS *Monitor*, the Civil War ironclad known to every schoolchild in America. *Monitor* is located off Cape Hatteras, North Carolina, in over two hundred feet of water. With the advances in diving and salvage technology, she is accessible and could, in fact, be recovered. But how? In what state? And at what cost? So that these questions can be answered, the ship has been protected legally by the creation of a surrounding "marine sanctuary" overseen by the National Oceanic and Atmospheric Administration, a federal agency. Subsequently, NOAA has organized two expeditions to the ship for purposes of photo-documentation and structural survey, has assembled numerous expert committees to study findings and address archaeological and conservation issues, and has assembled an impressive amount of historical data related to the ship, her crew, and her social context. *Monitor* may or may not be raised from the ocean floor. But she will nevertheless tell her story.

These are dramatic examples. But there are also thousands of other, less notorious maritime artifacts that can yield information of equal importance. The states of Maryland and South Carolina have begun systematic surveys of their waterways, mapping wrecks and recovering items when appropriate. Vermont has accomplished some extremely valuable work, including scholarly publications, almost entirely with the assistance of volunteer divers provided with archaeological training. As this knowledge expands, some wrecks will be recovered, in whole or in part; some may be studied and then left to nature; still others will be found without significance. In Florida and elsewhere, certain underwater areas, wrecks included, have been designated public "parks" for the use and enjoyment of sport divers.

Why Preserve Maritime America?

I was born in middle America, by a river but as equidistant from our three coasts as is physically possible. I can remember vividly the day my father first took me to visit the ocean, a rocky beach in Gloucester, Massachusetts, where a gusting wind and the ticking of stones rolling in the surf added a degree of reality to the literary descriptions in the Hornblower books and other sea novels on which I had previously relied. I did not run off from St. Louis to become a cabin boy, but like so many others, so many of you, I felt the power of the water. What is it? And why is it that, poets excepted, so few of us try to articulate the reasons for this collective identification with the sea?

The sea constitutes challenge. Like history, it is volatile and ever-changing, at one moment innocent, at the next explosive and terrifying. It has never been our ability to tame the sea, but rather to exist successfully upon the water, a response that can only be measured by competence. Knots, for example; every seaman must know them, must be able to tie them in the dead of night or, aloft, in the midst of a raging storm. Knots are, of course, remarkable human responses to recurring situations at sea, both symbol and reality of a seaman's competence. The survival of the vessel and her entire crew can depend on the integrity of a single knot.

So, too, the ships themselves, each a more sophisticated response to the needs of those who manned them. The dugout canoe, the shallow draft coaster, the Grand Banks schooner, the clipper ship—each of these, and many others, had a purpose, a utilitarian link to the work they were to perform. Shape, size, means of power; each was based on the task to be met, and today, when we look at a boat, whether with knowing or unknowing eye, the beauty we see is an evocation of sublime function.

The origin of our maritime heritage is found in *work*, a tradition of admirable accomplishment defined by the efforts of men and women, past and present, on and by the sea. Boats are tools; like an axe or adze or caulking mallet, they are only as good as the hands that wield them. As the crews ranged farther at sea, their dependence on others increased. Those who stayed at home, the craftsmen and builders, were part of the passage, responsible for the safety of the watermen by the success—or devastating failure—of their handiwork.

Essential to our maritime heritage, then, is this sense of connection. The seaman is connected to the quality of his ship and tools, to the crew with whom he works exhausting hours, and to family life and community custom, art, song, religion. This link is readily apparent in photographs of men furling sails in a blow off Cape Horn, just as it is in the teamwork among the crew of an America's Cup yacht. It is apparent in the system of apprenticeship whereby a father taught a son, a captain taught a crew, a crewman taught another, passing on the skills in a manner not much different than that of the Sound School program. The sense of connection is apparent in the meeting houses of whaling Nantucket, just as it is in the annual "blessing of the fleet" in our modern fishing ports.

But, above all, the seaman relies upon himself. Self-knowledge, competence, experience, humility in the face of immeasurable force and omnipresent danger; these are the attributes upon which he must depend. A strong current of individualism ran, and runs still today, through the marine trades, an independence of mind and decisiveness resulting from acceptance of responsibility for self and others. Now, as then, life at sea is as complex, as challenging, as life ashore, but onboard there is no room for psychiatrists, no time for much but action, no evasion of work or accountability—in short, conditions that, as that great sailor, Irving Johnson, once wrote, insist that one "lean forward into life."

Throughout history, we have left safe havens on journeys of exploration into an unknown characterized by strange monsters, whirlpools, and storms that approached the wrath of God. Like the desert, like the mountainous wild, the sea was, and remains, a beautiful mystery, a place for human adventure, a scape of light and dark and changing color, of profound passion, mystical emptiness, constant sound, and eternal motion. Now and forever, the sea overwhelms our reason and our senses and we are *connected*.

10
The Sea Education Association operates the schooner Westward *as a research vessel. The ship is manned by students enrolled in accredited college courses in marine biology and oceanography. The ship's ambitious itinerary of research stations ranges from Nova Scotia to the Bahamas. The program is an outstanding example of present-day manifestations of maritime America.*

THE PEABODY MUSEUM OF SALEM

The Peabody Museum of Salem

SALEM · MASSACHUSETTS

Originally named Naumkeag, Salem had long been settled by American Indians when Roger Conant and a group of colonists from Cape Ann migrated to the area in 1626. Within two decades of its founding, Salem's shipbuilders were constructing vessels of up to three hundred tons for trade to the southern colonies, West Indies, and Europe. In 1683, the town became one of the region's two lawful ports of entry for foreign cargoes, and by 1700 the local fleet had grown to approximately one hundred vessels ranging from little shallops, ketches, and schooners to oceangoing brigs and ships. Long wharves lined with warehouses, shops, and merchants' countinghouses reached out into the harbor's busy waters, and the streets were filled with merchants, sea captains, shipbuilders, coopers, sail and cordage makers, chandlers, blacksmiths, innkeepers, and common seamen. Virtually the town's entire population contributed directly or indirectly to the local sea-based commerce.

Until the American Revolution, Salem's maritime enterprise was marked by consolidation and gradual expansion. Occasional brushes with French or British privateers during the wars between the period's superpowers and frequent trade acts imposed on the colonies by the mother country cut into the immense profits to be made by the most daring and industrious mariners, but these factors did not dampen Salem's entrepreneurial spirit. Gradually, Salem's fleet was consolidated under the control of around two dozen merchant-shipowners with names like English, Orne, Derby, Pickman, and Crowninshield. Many of them founded merchant dynasties, with family members crewing their ships, staffing their countinghouses, and taking on cultural and political responsibilities within the community and region.

During the Revolution, the carefully nurtured local maritime enterprise suffered greatly from the disruption of normal trading routes and patterns. The British naval

11
Preceding pages:
The Scottish artist Robert Salmon (ca. 1775–1845) emigrated to the United States in 1828 at the age of 53. Less than five years later, in 1832, he painted the waterfront at Chelsea, Massachusetts, as seen from Boston, prior to the Medford Street District development. On the right is the popular Taft Tavern, located at the old Ferry Ways. Shortly after this scene was painted, the Winnesimet Company inaugurated a steam ferry service from Chelsea to Boston.

12
For 25 years, the Peabody Museum's founding captain-collectors, the East India Marine Society, operated the museum in rented quarters. In 1824, the society commissioned Boston architect Thomas Waldron Sumner to design their first permanent building, East India Marine Hall. Completed in 1825, the Federal-style building became a Registered National Historic Landmark in 1966. This view shows a line of figureheads along the southern side of the hall.

13

blockade, privateering, and impressment combined to make Salem's trade riskier and less profitable. The merchants retaliated by developing new sources for trade, by smuggling and by converting their merchant vessels into privateers and preying on the British shipping in New England's waters. Success in this particular enterprise allowed several individuals to prosper in the postrevolutionary period, having amassed considerable fleets and fortunes during the conflict. No fewer than 458 British prize vessels were captured by Salem's 158 privateers.

The period between the Revolution and the War of 1812 has been justly called Salem's golden age. No longer were the town's merchants restricted by trade laws, and by 1800 the ships of Salem were in every major port of the globe, from Archangel to Zanzibar. In exchange for New England's rum, fish, timber, munitions, and other products, daring captains brought back silks, ivory, spices, gold, tea, coffee, porcelains, wine, hides, textiles, and many more exotic cargoes from the far reaches of the world's waters. Profits against investment could range as high as 700 percent, and more than one ship paid for her construction, fitting out, crew, and cargo in a single voyage. The prosperity engendered by Salem's vast trading empire continued unabated until first the Jeffersonian Embargo of 1807 and then the War of 1812 cut into the city's seaborne commerce. However, it was during Salem's heyday that the East India Marine Society, which founded the Peabody Museum of Salem, was born.

13
This period room at the Peabody Museum is a reconstruction of the main saloon of Cleopatra's Barge, *the first deep-water yacht ever built in the United States. Patterned after* America, *the most successful privateer in the War of 1812, the* Barge *was constructed at Salem in 1816 for George Crowninshield, Jr., at a cost of nearly $100,000. After a singularly bizarre pleasure voyage to the Mediterranean, Crowninshield died, and his family stripped the hermaphrodite brig of her fittings and furnishings. In 1820, King Kamehameha II of Hawaii purchased the* Barge *for 8,000 piculs of sandalwood and converted her into his royal yacht,* Haaheo o Hawaii (Pride of Hawaii). *On April 5, 1924, while the king and one of his wives were in London, the* Barge *was wrecked at the island of Kauai. Either the captain or the entire crew except the captain was drunk.*

14

14
*The Peabody Museum of Salem, from
East India Square. To the left of the
Oriental Garden is East India Marine
Hall. On the far left is the Ernest
Stanley Dodge Wing, completed and
dedicated in 1976.*

The East India Marine Society
and the Museum of Captain-Collectors

Founded in 1799 as the East India Marine Society, the Peabody Museum of Salem is the oldest maritime museum in the United States. Marine societies were an eighteenth-century phenomenon common to port cities along the eastern seaboard. Generally charitable in nature, such societies provided for the welfare of the families of seamen lost in the pursuit of their profession or suffering from financial hardship. "To collect such facts and observations as may tend to the improvement and security of navigation" indicates the other main objective of these organizations: to form archives of useful navigational information. The East India Marine Society's reputation was greatly enhanced by its association with the scientific sailor Nathaniel Bowditch (1773–1838), author of *The New American Practical Navigator*, keeper of journals and president of the society from 1820 to 1823. So well known were the resources of the society that the sailing orders of Captain Charles Wilkes, commander of the American exploring expedition to the Pacific from 1838 to 1842, contained specific instructions to consult the files of the society for information.

15

15
Through the use of a library captured from a British prize vessel by a Beverly privateer during the American Revolution, Salem mathematician and astronomer Nathaniel Bowditch (1773–1838) was entirely self-educated. In 1802, he first published The New American Practical Navigator, *which is still in use today in an updated edition. In later life, Bowditch declined professorships at Harvard, West Point, and the University of Virginia to become the nation's first insurance actuary. This 1835 portrait by Charles Osgood depicts the scientific sailor at work on his internationally acclaimed translation of* Mécanique Céleste *by the Marquis de la Place. The bust of the marquis watches over Bowditch's labors from the upper left.*

16
America's first millionaire, Elias Hasket Derby (1739–99) is unique among Salem's merchant princes for not having gone to sea. After the Revolution, during which he made a fortune from a fleet of successful privateers, Derby converted his vessels to merchantmen and spearheaded the new nation's trade in the Baltic region, the East Indies, China, and the Philippines. James Frothingham's posthumous portrait of Derby at the height of his powers displays the merchant's most unusual physical attributes: one brown eye and one blue eye. The ship in the background is the famous Grand Turk *of Salem, the first New England vessel in China.*

16

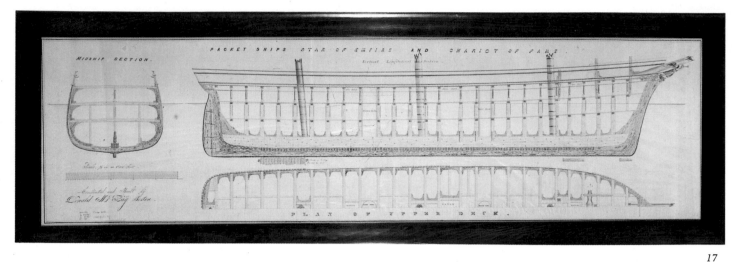

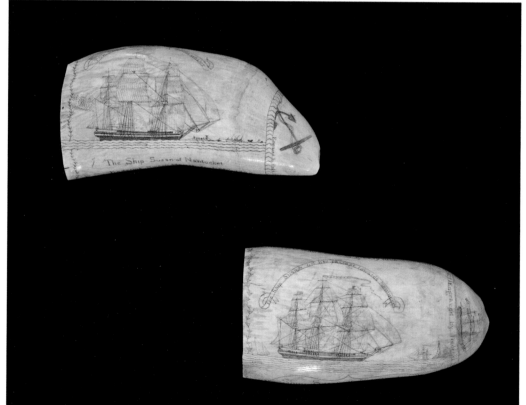

17
These rare construction plans of the sister ships Chariot of Fame *and* Star of Empire *are in the hand of New England's most famous clipper ship builder, Donald McKay of East Boston. Both of the medium clippers were built in 1853 for the Boston packet company of Enoch Train & Co., which used them in the Boston–Liverpool service. Chariot's career is fairly typical for a clipper. Early on she served as a packet for two sets of owners. Later, she was a general cargo carrier, a guano ship, a China trader, and a Gold Rush vessel. She dropped out of the international shipping registers in 1873.*

18
Carved aboard the Nantucket whaleship Susan *by artist Frederick Myrick during a lengthy Pacific voyage that lasted from 1826 to 1829, so-called "Susan's Teeth" are the earliest signed and dated pieces of American scrimshaw. Of the Peabody Museum's three examples, two are dated January 1829 and are listed in the museum's 1831 catalog as Nos. 4282 and 4283, "Tooth of a Sperm Whale, curiously carved" and "Another, carved by the same hand."*

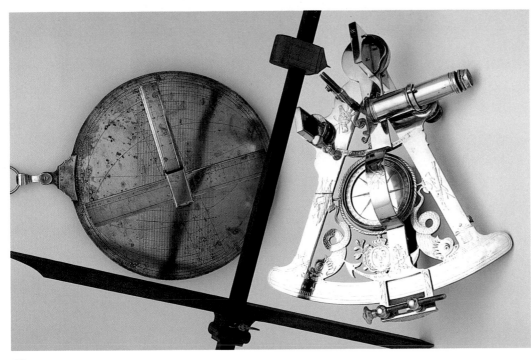

19

20

19

Highlights of the Peabody Museum's collection of navigating instruments include an early-18th-century American wooden cross staff, an early-17th-century astrolabe that once belonged to Nathaniel Bowditch, and a late-18th-century French octant specially made by Magnié for King Louis XVI and heavily encrusted with decorative elements.

20

The extreme clipper ship Flying Cloud *was the fastest commercial sailing vessel ever built. Constructed in 1851 by Donald McKay at East Boston, Massachusetts,* Cloud *is best remembered for her two 89-day record passages from New York to San Francisco via Cape Horn under command of Josiah Perkins Creesy of Marblehead. Among the Peabody's collections relating to this vessel are Captain Creesy's abstracted log of the 1851 maiden, record-breaking voyage, his speaking trumpet, an original sailing card, a straight edge made of African ironwood taken from the bowsprit when* Flying Cloud *was broken up at St. John's, New Brunswick, in June 1875, and a contemporary painting by John C. Wade of the ship loading at New York. Among more recent acquisitions is a commemorative postcard issued out of the Peabody Museum by the United States Post Office on February 27, 1985.*

Unlike other marine societies, however, the East India Marine Society included in its charter the decision to form a "museum of natural and artificial curiosities, particularly such as are to be found beyond the Cape of Good Hope and Cape Horn." Such curiosity stemmed from the expeditions of Samuel Wallace, Louis Antoine de Bougainville, and, most famous of all, the voyages of Captain James Cook, which did much to create excitement about the newly discovered lands in the Pacific and the "noble savages" encountered there. It was no accident that in ports like Salem, Captain Cook's name was well known; his portrait was the first to be commissioned by the Society in 1803.

Like Captain Cook, who brought scientists and artists on his voyages, so would members of the East India Marine Society return from their voyages with natural and

artificial—or, in today's terms, ethnographic—specimens from the far corners of a world already circumnavigated countless times. The blank journals that Nathaniel Bowditch issued to society members would result in over one hundred records of voyages that detailed navigational, meteorological, and cultural observations as well as data on local methods and customs of trade. These collectors, however, were not artists or scientists, for the marine society required only that they be captains or supercargoes of vessels that sailed beyond the Cape of Good Hope or Cape Horn. From 1799 to the mid-nineteenth century, there were over three hundred members who brought back and recorded in their catalog gifts to the society's museum. Objects from the Pacific, China, Japan, Java, Sumatra, India, Africa, Arabia, Zanzibar, Madagascar, Mauritius, the Mediterranean, and

22
The earliest model of the frigate USS Constitution *("Old Ironsides") was presented by her commander Isaac Hull to the Salem East India Marine Society during the War of 1812, only a few months after the frigate's victories over the British warships* Guerriere *and* Java. *Shortly after the formal donation, at one of the society's regular banquets at which some 80 spirited toasts were offered, it was decided to float the model in a tub of water and set off the deck cannon as a salute. To the astonishment and dismay of the somewhat inebriated group of distinguished society members, the model caught on fire and the rigging was badly damaged. The embarrassing situation was ultimately rectified by sending the model to a prison ship in Salem Harbor, where it was repaired by British prisoners of war at a cost of $12.*

the Baltic formed the nucleus of the Peabody Museum's renowned ethnographic and export collections.

By 1850, nearly all of the original members of the East India Marine had passed away, and replacements for them were hard to find in Salem, by this time a distant backwater to the ports of Boston and New York. As a result, it became increasingly difficult to keep the museum's doors open. By the mid-1860s, the society members, now the sons of the original captains and supercargoes, were forced to entertain the prospect of selling the collections to replenish the dwindling treasury. In 1867, however, an unexpected benefactor in England stepped forward and endowed a trust to preserve the collections intact. This philanthropist was George Peabody, a native of Essex County, Massachusetts, who had emigrated to London and become a successful banker. Com-

23

memorating Peabody's generosity, the museum was renamed the Peabody Academy of Science, the name it retained until 1915 when it received its present name.

Maritime history first achieved formal recognition at the Peabody Museum in January 1905, with the opening of the Marine Room and its display of ship, captain, and merchant portraits, ship models, and related memorabilia. This exhibit, drawing together resources already in the collections but previously considered "of everyday knowledge and therefore not appropriate," was the first maritime history exhibit in the country. By 1921, the marine collections were large enough to be published in a special guidebook, and four years later they acquired their first curator. Today they are among the world's finest gatherings of maritime historical materials.

23
From 1837 to 1840, French explorer Jules-Sébastien-César Dumont d'Urville (1790–1842) led two expeditions to the southern hemisphere to investigate Pacific and Antarctic waters. The painting by the official expedition artist Louis Le Breton depicts Dumont d'Urville's two ships L'Astrolabe *and* La Zelée *stranded at the Torres Strait between Australia and New Guinea in May and June 1840.*

The Letter of marque Brig Grand Turk of 14 Guns W.m Austin Com.er Saluting Marseilles.

The Collections

Published in 1821, the museum's earliest printed catalog lists a pair of New Zealand paddles as the first maritime acquisition. During the nineteenth century, ship captains were reluctant to allow their crewmen ashore lest they desert or find themselves in even less savory situations. As a result, the museum's early collections are filled with the sorts of things that sailors might obtain from natives visiting the foreign ships in their local watercraft. Numbers 159–170 in the 1821 catalog were assigned to boat models from Japan to Nova Scotia, indicating an intense interest on the part of the society membership in the maritime customs of foreign cultures, if not their own. As already mentioned, in 1803 the society commissioned its first portrait, and the first formal ship portraits appear in the 1821 catalog as numbers 357–375. Western and Pacific navigating

24
The armed brig Grand Turk *of Salem was one of the most successful letter-of-marque vessels during the War of 1812, capturing a total of 39 British ships over the course of five voyages. Built as a privateer at Wiscasset, Maine,* Turk *was purchased by a cartel of 30 Salem entrepreneurs and named after the first New England vessel in China. After the war ended,* Turk *was sold to Salem merchant William Gray. On her first trading voyage to the Mediterranean,* Grand Turk *entered Marseilles harbor and fired a salute, an event captured by local marine artist Anton Roux.*

The Mount Vernon of Salem comanded by Capt. J. Elias Derby = 1789 m.c.

25

instruments, ships' porcelain, fishing tools, naval relics, ordnance, and the like also fill the pages of this early listing of museum resources.

The sailor's art of scrimshaw first appears in the 1831 edition of the catalog as "Sperm whale's teeth, curiously carved." Signed in 1829 by artist Frederick Myrick aboard the Nantucket whaleship *Susan*, the museum received them within one year of their having been carved. The gathering of such traditional categories of maritime artifacts as paintings, prints, ship models, charts, logbooks, navigating instruments, scrimshaw, tools, and the like may seem obvious to the museums of today, but 150 years ago Salem's captain-collectors were setting the standards for the collections of all American maritime museums.

25
The ship Mount Vernon *was built at Salem in 1798 by Retire Becket for merchant Elias Hasket Derby. Clearing Salem in July 1799,* Mount Vernon *spent nine months trading in the Mediterranean, narrowly escaping capture by French privateers several times. Upon her return to Salem in 1800,* Mount Vernon's *cargo netted a profit of $100,000 on an initial investment of $40,000. This voyage also brought the Neapolitan marine painter Michele Felice Cornè to these shores, and the artist painted more than two dozen pictures of the Derby ship in 1799 and 1800, evidently in exchange for his passage.*

Sometimes the marine interests and curiosity of these deepwater seamen strayed from more traditional artifacts. Thus, for example, the early catalogs dutifully record several fragments of bricks from Christopher Columbus's birthplace in Genoa, chips of Plymouth Rock, and petrified clams from a deep hole on a Sicilian mountaintop. A taste for the macabre is manifest in such items as garments made from the intestines of various sea mammals, a journal kept in blood on a sealskin by sailors accidentally marooned on a desolate South Sea island, and fragments of the rock in Hawaii where Captain Cook was killed. Words occasionally failed the fastidious museum staff diligently recording the year's accessions, as seen in the 1831 catalog listing of "A Speaking Trumpet, made from a part of a (male) whale," and "A substance brought up on an Anchor from the Chinese Seas." Although they were authorities on seamanship and trade, the society members were not always serious collectors, and they could be fooled. The 1831 catalog lists two sphinx larvae and two separate gifts of rubber alligators.

From these early beginnings grew the Peabody Museum's core collections; today, those horizons continue to expand in several directions. East India Marine Hall, the museum's first permanent building, was completed and occupied in 1825; in 1966, it became a Registered National Historic Landmark. The Ernest S. Dodge wing was built in 1976, nearly doubling the museum's exhibition and storage space. In 1984, the Alexander O. Vietor Conservation Laboratory opened its doors, and in the same year the Museum of the American China Trade merged with the Peabody Museum, forming the world's most extensive collections of Asian Export Art and artifacts. A new wing exhibits the combined collections of the two institutions. In less than a dozen years, the Peabody Museum of Salem will enter its third century of continuous operation, reflecting both its longstanding maritime legacy as well as looking forward to the future enrichment and appreciation of that historic element of our national heritage.

26
The nation's most renowned marine artist is Fitz Hugh Lane (1804–65), a native of Gloucester, Massachusetts, and one of the foremost members of the American Luminist movement. Although he never left this hemisphere, Lane painted this oil of the schooner yacht America *at Cowes, England, in 1851, using a sketch by Oswald W. Brierly as his model. The picture shows* America *winning the Royal Yacht Club Cup in 1851, an event better known as the first America's Cup.*

26

THE KENDALL WHALING MUSEUM

2 *"The High and Mighty Business of Whaling": A Handful of Treasures from the Kendall Whaling Museum*
Stuart M. Frank, Director

The Kendall Whaling Museum

SHARON · MASSACHUSETTS

The Kendall Whaling Museum, founded in Sharon, Massachusetts, in 1956, houses a distinctively international collection of whaling artworks, artifacts, and archival resources spanning six centuries and seven continents. While maritime museums have typically concerned themselves with the seafaring heritage of a single nation, locale, or historical epoch, the Kendall Whaling Museum, perhaps uniquely, has taken a polyglot view of a single maritime industry—regarded in its many historical and cultural facets without nationalistic or temporal limitation and including such ancillary aspects as prehistory, literature, natural-history illustration, and the whale preservation movement. Thus, while its conventional American and Native North American holdings are among the finest anywhere, a broad cultural diversity and international emphasis provide as context the rich panoply of the age-old human encounter with the Leviathan.

As Herman Melville observes in *Moby-Dick:* ". . . The high and mighty business of whaling . . . has begotten events so remarkable in themselves, and so continuously momentous in their sequential issues, that . . . it would be a hopeless, endless task to catalogue all these things. Let a handful suffice." In this instance, our handful will consist of a selection from the earliest and most sumptuous manifestation of European whaling art, a component of the Kendall Whaling Museum's collection that most distinguishes it from other maritime collections in North America.

The history of whaling among European peoples, the ancestral precursor of the classic Yankee whale hunt of the nineteenth century, begins in the remote recesses of the so-called Dark Ages, when whales were hunted locally by Vikings on the coast of Norway and by Basques in the Bay of Biscay. While there is evidence to suggest that these fisheries were undertaken prior to the tenth century, little is known about their prosecution. Contemporaneous chroniclers only rarely mentioned whaling at all; nor did there emerge any pictorial tradition to illustrate the whale hunt in any of its ancient incarnations. Even

27
Preceding pages: *"The Whale beached between Scheveningen and Katwijk on 20 or 21 January 1617, with elegant sightseers,"* by Esaias van den Velde (1587–1630), ca. 1617

28
Detail from *"Three Whaleships of Zaandam on the Greenland Grounds,"* anonymous, ca. 1772, depicted in its entirety in Figure 33

the Basques, who perhaps as early as the fourteenth century and certainly by the sixteenth were already traversing the Atlantic to hunt whales seasonally on the coast of Labrador, did not develop such votive or decorative arts as might have illuminated for posterity details of their extraordinary whaling adventures. It was not until the age of exploration in the late Renaissance, with the secularization of the arts and sciences in northern Europe toward the end of the sixteenth century, that the whales that periodically washed ashore, those sighted at sea by North Atlantic and Arctic voyagers, and those taken by Basque mariners off Canada began to arrest the attention and interest of chroniclers, illustrators, and merchant entrepreneurs in Holland and England. It was under their influence and auspices that the first true commercial whale fishery was undertaken in the early seventeenth century.

"Ships and Whales in a Tempest" (fig. 31), painted circa 1595, stands at the head of the Netherlandish tradition of "realistic" marine painting commensurate with the rise of Dutch nationalism and maritime prowess; together with rival England, Holland would successfully challenge Spanish colonial authority in Europe and Iberian supremacy in the New World. The painting was formerly in the eminent collection of Sir Henry Ingram, who attributed it to Hendrik Cornelisz Vroom (ca. 1566–1640). Widely regarded as the founder of both the Dutch and Flemish schools of marine artists, Vroom is credited with having originated the faithful depiction of plausible naval architecture, a departure from the fancifully stylized ships of Hieronymus Bosch and Pieter Bruegel the Elder—albeit a

29

29
Dutch Gallery of the Kendall Whaling Museum showing rare contemporaneous folk model of a whaling fluyt *of the mid-17th century, domestic furniture of the 17th century, a tall clock by Gerrit Knip of Amsterdam, and marine paintings by Dutch masters*

30
"Dutch Bay Whaling at Spitsbergen,"
by Cornelis Claesz van Wieringen
(1580–1633), ca. 1620. A member of
the Guild of Haarlem, van Wieringen
had been a sailor in his youth and a
pupil of H. C. Vroom

31
"Ships and Whales in a Tempest,"
school of H. C. Vroom, ca. 1595. One
of the earliest and finest marine
paintings of its type in North America

relative sort of realism, in this picture more evident with respect to the ships than to the whales. Working in his native Haarlem, during various travels through the Low Countries, Italy, France, and Spain, and at studios established successively at Haarlem, Leiden, and Antwerp, he trained many of the leading lights of the next generation of Netherlandish marine painters. In England he was commissioned to prepare the cartoons for a series of tapestries commemorating the destruction of the Spanish Armada of 1588—an event that symbolizes perhaps better than any other the northward shift of the axis of European commerce and culture, from the Mediterranean to the North Sea. Here, merchantmen flaunt an early version of the Dutch tricolor which, fifteen or twenty years hence, would be carried to the Arctic whaling grounds and to North America. When independence was finally achieved in the middle of the seventeenth century, this flag (with the pale orange changed to red) would acquire official status as the national ensign of the Dutch Republic.

Two paintings and a host of etchings and engravings identify one of the most peculiar and tenacious aspects of human fascination with whales which, in that era, contributed significantly to Dutch popular and scientific interest in cetaceans. Stranded whales have been known since time immemorial, and may in fact have been the genesis of the whale hunt in Europe and elsewhere; but beginning in 1577, it was the Dutch who established a pictorial record of major strandings—some realistically and others fancifully

32
"Sperm Whale Stranded on the North Sea Coast," by Adam Willaerts (1577–1664)

33
"Three Whaleships of Zaandam on the Greenland Grounds," anonymous, ca. 1772. The vessels are clearly identifiable from names on the sternboards, the William *(left), the* Anna *(center), and* De Jacob *(right). All were Greenland whalers of Zaandam active in the 1770s.*

33

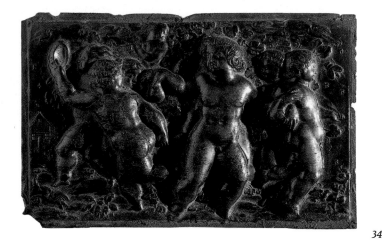

34
"Bacchanalian Frolic," pressed baleen panel attributed to Jan Lutma the Elder (ca. 1584–1669) and Jan Osborn (ca. 1581–1643), ca. 1618–41. Surviving examples in this medium are extremely rare. Most are portraits of the gentry or the Dutch royal family.

35
"Ship Hollandia *Whaling in Company on the Arctic Grounds" by Abram van Salm of Delftshaven (fl. ca. 1670–1720), ca. 1702. Monochrome penschildering (pen-painting) or grisaille (gray painting) on panel. Abram van Salm and his son Roelf (or Reynier) often utilized this medium in the whaling genre.*

36
"Greenland Whale Fishery." Ensemble of 80 monochrome manganese faience tiles, 18th century. After the double-folio etching "Groenlandsche Visschery" (Greenland Whale Fishery) drawn by Sieuwert van der Meulen (d. 1730), etched by Adolph van der Laan (1684–1742), and published ca. 1720 in Amsterdam by Petrus Schenck

rendered—that remained virtually unbroken for the ensuing two and a half centuries. Not that many of the later depictions were entirely original: by the 1590s the genre had begun to attract some of Holland's most accomplished printmakers, notably Hendrik Goltzius (1558–1617); Jacob Matham (1571–1631), who based his definitive engraving of a 1598 stranding upon Goltzius's prototype; and Jan Saenrendam (1565–1607), whose baroque rendering of 1602 imparts elaborate symbolism to an event that was increasingly taken to signify a great deal more than merely the coming ashore of a large sea animal. The work of these three engravers (with a few additions from natural-history illustrators Conrad von

Gesner and Ulysses Aldrovandus) formed the basic canon of stranded-whale types from which most subsequent illustrators copied.

Despite the proliferation of such prints throughout Europe, contemporaneous oil paintings of such strandings are quite rare; strictly defined, only three are known. Two of these are in the Kendall Whaling Museum, both by Flemish masters working in Holland and both based on prints by Matham (after Goltzius), but each has original components as well as its own vision and emphasis. Of the three, the earliest is an anonymous oil painting entitled "Whale beached at Brouwershaven, on the Springersplaat [in the Scheldt delta of

37

37

37
*"Japanese Whaling," woodblock
print by Kuniyoshi (1797–1861), ca.
1840. Japanese whaling is known
today primarily in connection with
modern floating-factory ships and the
controversy surrounding the possible
extermination of entire species through
overfishing. Traditional Japanese
hand-whaling began in coastal
villages of Honshu in the 16th
century. It inspired formal conventions
of painting and scroll illustration in
the 1700s and was a subject adopted
by some of the leading printmakers of
Japan's great 19th-century florescence
of the arts.*

Flanders] 1606," in the collection of the Rijksmuseum van Natuurlijke Historie at Leiden; there is a replica at the Stadhuis of Brouwershaven, and Prof. Els van Eyck van Heslinga reports another in a private collection at Leiden. "The Whale beached between Scheveningen and Katwijk on 20 or 21 January 1617, with elegant sightseers" (fig. 27), a large work on canvas by Esaias van den Velde (1587–1630), is the more orthodox of the two at the Kendall, with the Matham-derived whale dominant, surrounded by curious onlookers in their Sunday finery and with the gentle curve of the Dutch coast suggesting a picturesqueness that fades into the sublimity of seascape. Only two boats are visible

alongshore, both rather sketchily drawn. Yet, during the recent restoration of this painting at the Fogg Museum of Harvard University, electronic scrutiny revealed a network of substrata evidencing many compositional and architectural changes during its execution, and testifying anew to the freshness and originality of van den Velde's interpretation of what was at the time a conventional subject.

The analogous work informally known as "Sperm Whale Stranded on the North Sea Coast" (fig. 32), rendered on a smaller panel by Adam Willaerts (1577–1664), takes a rather different view of the same subject. While van den Velde's title could as easily apply

38

39

40

38

"Whaling in the Polar Sea," by Ludolf Backhuyzen (1631–1708), ca. 1700. The brightly painted golden whale on the carved sternboard of the principal vessel (right) indicates that this is De Vergulde Walvis (The Golden Whale), a Greenlander of Amsterdam, the most famous of several whaleships to bear this name successively. This vessel also flies the Dutch tricolor emblazoned with a black right whale, a traditional but unofficial ensign on the whaling grounds.

39

"Whaleship Frankendaal of Amsterdam, Maarten Mooy of Callantsoog, Master, Whaling in Company on the Greenland Grounds, 1786," by Jan Mooy (1776–1847), signed and dated 1843. Based on a narrative that was written by Maarten Mooy, the artist's father, and published in Amsterdam in 1787. The narrative detailed Captain Mooy's voyage of 1786 as commander of the Frankendaal, one of his many seasons whaling in the Arctic. The principal vessels are (left) De Jager (The Hunter), the (center) Groenlandia, and the (second from right) Frankendaal.

40

"British Whaling in the Arctic," by John Carmichael (1800–68). British whaling in the Arctic commenced about 1610, prior to the Dutch fishery, but it was more than a century before English artists challenged the virtual Dutch monopoly of whaling art. At first derivative from Dutch prototypes, the British whaling genre came into its own in the 19th century. Carmichael's painting is notable not only for its stirring action and vivid color but also for representing the whaling fleet of Newcastle-upon-Tyne, the artist's birthplace.

to Willaerts's work as his own, the Willaerts rendition is in a more complete sense a true "marine" painting. Willaerts creates a more panoramic perspective, with the whale (also derived from Matham) reduced in size and thus in relative importance with respect to the whole; there is less emphasis upon the gentry and their activities, and more upon the variety of recognizable types of watercraft alongshore, each of which is drafted with great accuracy and attention to detail.

A magnificently panoramic painting by Cornelis Claesz van Wieringen (1580–1633) depicting Dutch bay whaling in the Arctic, circa 1620 (fig. 30), is of monumental significance both as an artistic milestone and as an historical document. In the flush of excitement generated by the northern voyages of Frobisher, Barendsz, and Hudson, British and Dutch entrepreneurs were not long in organizing expeditions to harvest the walruses and whales widely reported to have populated the newly discovered Arctic regions. Van Wieringen's picture, rendered scarcely a decade after seasonal whaling voyages were first undertaken from London and Amsterdam, is likely the first oil painting of a pelagic whaling scene; more important, it is encyclopedic in its documentation of whaling in this early incarnation. Not many years after it was painted, permanent buildings replaced the storage tents visible here and, owing to the depletion of whale stocks in the protected bays inshore, the hunt itself was forced gradually offshore among the ice floes of the open sea. Seasonal stations like this one at Spitsbergen, in the extreme North Atlantic, increasingly became encampments for provisioning and processing rather than as sites of the whale-hunting activity itself. Among the many superlative features of van Wieringen's rendering are portraits of early forms of whaling watercraft, the ships being generic Dutch oceangoing types antecedent to any special adaptations for whaling, and the boats sporting Basque-influenced *fleur-de-lis* decorations. The presence of Basque harpooneers and flensing masters—identifiable by their berets and Iberian costume—is also significant. Basques were employed by the British and the Dutch for their invaluable skill and experience with whaling methods, at the time (and unique to Basque culture) already generations old.

Dutch commercial and cultural florescence in the seventeenth century, fueled by the inpouring of wealth from burgeoning fisheries and a thriving deepwater trade, made its mark on whaling as well as on virtually every facet of daily affairs. Artists and artisans vigorously exploited the decorative possibilities in the new market created by whaling merchants, entrepreneurs, and *commandeurs* (whaling masters) who would surround themselves with the symbols and trappings of their successes.

Some of the innovations were intended to be as practical as they were beautiful. Under license from the Northern Company, which monopolized Dutch whaling from 1614 to 1641 and was interested in turning a surplus of baleen ("whalebone") to some profitable purpose, English-born Jan Osborn and Dutch silversmith Jan Lutma the Elder attempted to develop a patented process for ornamental pressed-baleen furniture panels that would provide a workable substitute for costly carved ebony. However, baleen proved to be structurally unsuitable, and relatively few such panels were produced; fewer still survive (fig. 34).

Abraham Storck (ca. 1635–1710) and Abram van Salm (active ca. 1670–1720) had more success turning out purely decorative whaling scenes at a high standard of technical accuracy; no whaling collection, then or now, can be counted truly complete without a typically Dutch *penschildering* (monochrome "pen-painting") by Salm (fig. 35).

41

41

''Vae Victis—The Cachalot Cutting-In,'' by William Edward Norton, ca. 1900. Norton (1843–1916) was born in Boston and was trained in anatomy at the Harvard Medical School and in painting by the great American impressionist George Inness. He served as a sailor before the mast, maintained studios at different times in London and Boston, and exhibited in Paris, London, Philadelphia, Chicago, and St. Louis.

42

42

Two anonymous examples of British whalemen's art from the post-Napoleonic period. Watercolor ''Ship Adam of London Sperm-Whaling in the South Seas,'' inscribed ''Adam of London,'' and a large scrimshaw sperm-whale tooth. Adam was built in Duxbury, Massachusetts, in 1795, and placed in service as the Nantucket ship Renown. It was taken as an Admiralty prize in 1813 while homeward bound under Captain Zaccheus Barnard with 1,600 barrels of sperm oil aboard. Renamed Adam and registered in London, the ship was again engaged in sperm whaling from 1815 until, outward bound in 1825, she was wrecked in a storm off Deal. The whale's tooth, engraved with a whaling scene, is formally inscribed: ''This is the tooth of a sperm whale that was caught near the Galapagos Islands by the crew of the ship Adam, and made 100 barrels of oil in the year 1817.''

The collaboration of painter-draftsman Sieuwart van der Meulen (d. 1730) and etcher-engraver Adolf van der Laan (1684–1742) resulted in a series of whaling and herring-fishery prints that were published in numerous Dutch and foreign editions throughout the eighteenth century. These became a kind of canon upon which subsequent artists and illustrators drew shamelessly, including the first generation of British whaling artists. The Meulen–Laan influence is nowhere more pronounced than in whaling pictures replicated in Dutch faïence—the so-called Delft blueware and manganese crockery and tiles produced in Holland since the early seventeenth century. Examples in the Kendall Whaling Museum include a rare series of twelve blueware dinner plates made in Delft circa 1761, and several ensembles of tiles; but the most spectacular is undoubtedly the eighty-tile panorama faithfully copied after an enormous Meulen–Laan etching of circa 1720 entitled "Groenlandsche Visschery" ("Greenland Whale Fishery"; fig. 36).

The Dutch whaling industry inspired a handsome profusion of decorative artworks. A whaleman's etched baleen box of circa 1631 (the companionpiece of a specimen in the Rijksmuseum, Amsterdam) anticipates what Yankee sperm-whalemen some two centuries later would call *scrimshaw*—itself a term that may have derived from old Dutch. Also rendered in the manner of the folk-practitioner, a rare contemporaneous model of a whaling *fluyt* of the mid-1600s (fig. 29) exaggerates the naval architecture and the

43
"A Tough Old Bull," by William Heysman Overend (1851–98). Sperm-whaling scene. A ship in the background flies the house flag of H. & J. French of Sag Harbor, Long Island.

44

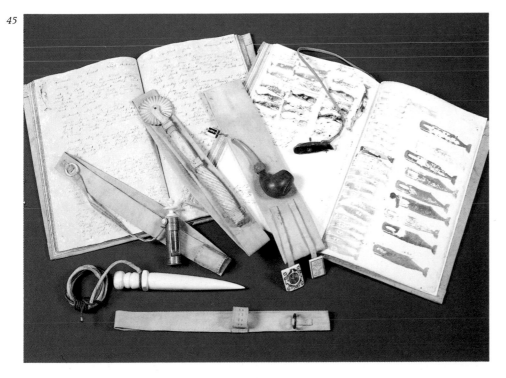

45

44

*American whaling memorabilia
(clockwise from upper left):* 20th-
century model, by Azorian-American
Manuel Pacheco Gamboa, of whaling
bark *Wanderer*, the last square-
rigged American whaler, wrecked on
Cuttyhunk Island, Massachusetts, in
1924; scrimshaw sewing box, ebony
trimmed with walrus ivory, with
walrus-ivory swift (yarn-winder),
19th century; three whaling irons
from New Bedford, mid-19th century;
Davis quadrant of ebony and
boxwood, made in 1758 by Benjamin
King of Newport for whaling captain
Ephraim Delano; scrimshaw whale's
teeth: the whaleship *L. C. Richmond*
of Bristol, Rhode Island, ca. 1834–37,
and a whaling scene with a hot air
balloon, inscribed (and attributed to)
Moses R. Denning, 19th century;
shipboard journal of a whaling voyage
on the *Lucy Ann* of Wilmington,
Henry King, master, kept by seaman
John F. Martin, profusely illustrated
with his own watercolors and ink
drawings (1841–44).*

45

*Shipboard paraphernalia of Frederick
Howland Smith of Dartmouth,
including scrimshaw he made and
journals he kept as a green hand,
seaman, harpooner, and officer on
whaling voyages on several New
Bedford vessels, 1854–74. Smith was
later a successful whaling master.*

features of animals emblematically portrayed on the carved sternboard. An anonymous oil-on-panel of Zaandam vessels whaling on Greenland, circa 1772, typifies whalemen's work (fig. 33); while a detailed whaling scene expertly engraved on glass by Jan Stam of Zaandam (ca. 1750–60), and a majestic tall clock of the same vintage with an elaborate mechanism by Gerrit Knip of Amsterdam (fig. 29), with ornamental whaling scenes, testify to the tenacity of whaling subjects among some of the most celebrated artisans and in some of the most fashionable homes of the eighteenth century.

This proliferation of whaling art does not appear to have degraded the academic genre. Notwithstanding significant variations in quality and emphasis among the many other Dutch and Flemish pictures in the Kendall Whaling Museum, the superb "Whaling in the Polar Sea" (fig. 38) was painted by Ludolf Backhuyzen (1631–1708) after the Amsterdam fishery had reached its economic high water mark. From the standpoints of technology and aesthetics, it is as proficient a work as any by this versatile master, leaving little doubt why Backhuyzen was selected to instruct Peter the Great in naval draftsmanship during the czar's pilgrimage to Holland. The watercolor "De Walvischvangst" ("Whaling"), painted about 1778 by Hendrik Kobell (1751–1779), and numerous engravings after Kobell by Mattheus de Sallieth (1749–1791), were produced when Dutch whaling was in serious decline. Jan Mooy (1776–1847) was the last Dutch artist to portray the fishery contemporaneously. Both versions of his famous Arctic whaling scene featuring the ship *Frankendaal* (fig. 39)—the analogue is in the Nederlands Scheepvaart Museum, Amsterdam—were painted in retrospect, long after the demise of the fishery itself, in nostalgic tribute to the artist's father, Maarten Mooy, master of the *Frankendaal*, whose service as an Arctic whaling commander spanned the remarkable tenure of thirty-five seasons.

The Dutch whaling epoch was but the first and most formalized incarnation of European whaling art. Not again would so high a proportion of a nation's best academicians and self-taught masters turn their hands to whaling themes in oil paint, watercolor, and printer's ink. Yet in the hands of their European and American successors, the genre would continue to flower and would continue to express the drama and fascination of the human encounter with the Leviathan. It would develop into something even closer to the life and labor of the whale hunters themselves, and closer to a respect for the vastness and authentic phenomena of nature—until in our present age, the commercial whale hunt has been rendered obsolete, and human sympathy has finally turned to favor the whale rather than the hunter.

46
"A Norwegian Steam Whaler striking his fish in the Varanger Fjord, July, 1882, as witnessed from the deck of the S.S. Yacht Pandora*," by George Earl, 1882. This scene was painted when the exclusive patent on mechanized Norwegian whaling was still held by its originator, Svend Foyn. With subsequent dramatic improvements in propulsion, naval architecture, and ordnance, this new technology would ultimately supplant the hand-whaling methods pioneered by the Vikings a millennium earlier.*

46

THE MYSTIC SEAPORT MUSEUM

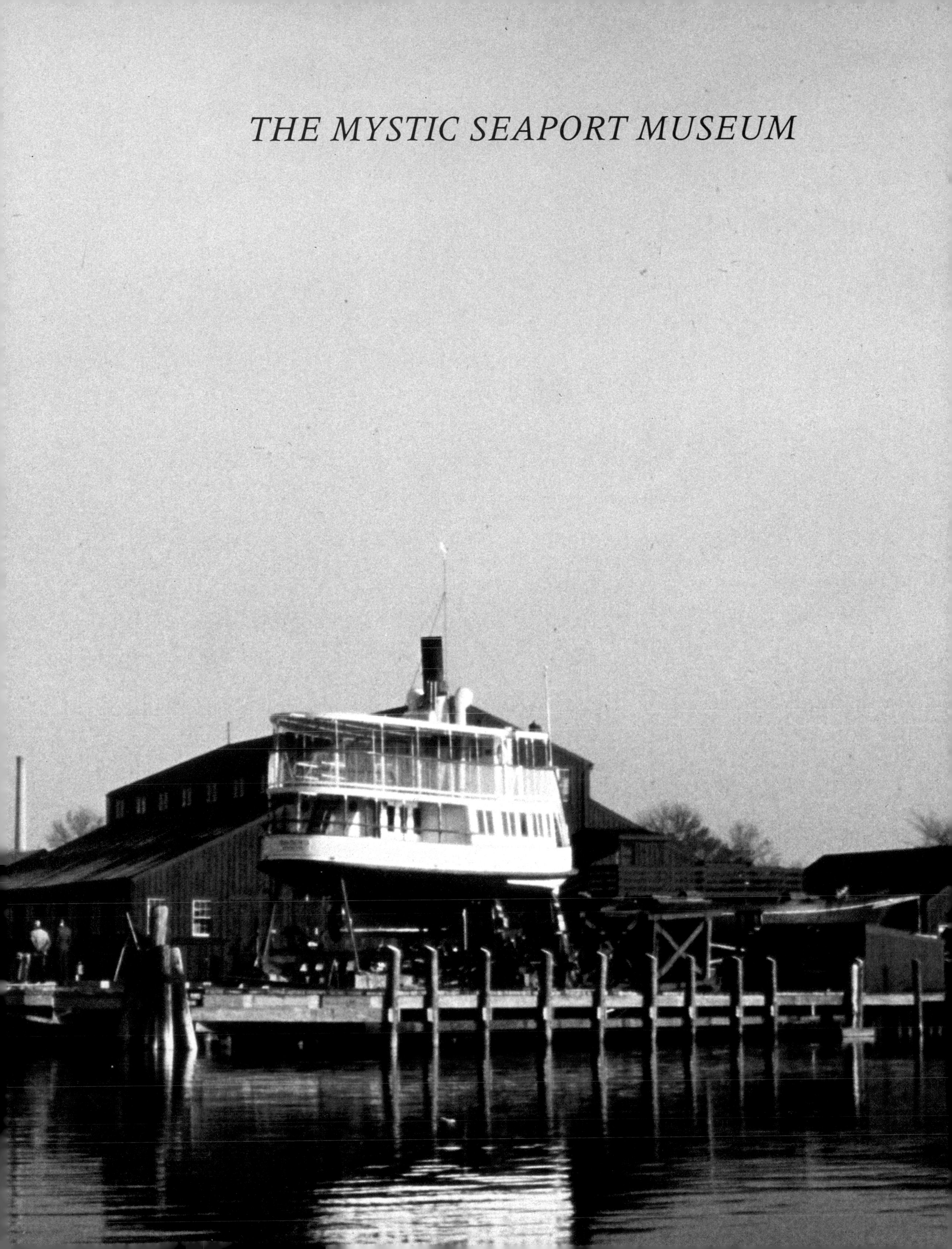

3 *Maritime Preservation at Mystic Seaport*
Andrew W. German,
Associate Editor

The Mystic Seaport Museum

MYSTIC · CONNECTICUT

From the ring of the caulker's mallet in the restoration shipyard to the ring of the anvil in the shipsmith shop to the ring of the ship's clock in an exhibit gallery, Mystic Seaport Museum preserves the artifacts, the knowledge, and the skills of America's maritime heritage. But when the three forward-looking custodians of maritime history, Carl C. Cutler, Edward E. Bradley, and Charles K. Stillman, assembled on Christmas Day, 1929, to found what is now Mystic Seaport, maritime preservation was barely recognized. A healthy, if not thriving, maritime economy was still a living memory for many coastal residents. Maritime artifacts might be treasured for their family associations, but in most cases they were ignored or even destroyed.

The founders hoped to counter this apathy toward the American maritime experience. Cutler and Bradley had been to sea, and Stillman was descended from Mystic shipbuilders. They had witnessed the decline of the merchant fleet and the thoughtless destruction of irreplaceable artifacts. Together they had a twofold dream: to preserve surviving elements of the nation's former maritime greatness, and to regenerate in America's youth the desire and the skills to perpetuate the merchant marine. With this nearly evangelistic vision, the founders were able to attract numerous members to their Marine Historical Association.

The museum's location in Mystic, Connecticut, was hardly an accident. Located between the prominent whaling port of New London and the sealing and fishing port of Stonington, Mystic itself has a long seafaring tradition. Mystic sons, such as Captain Joseph Warren Holmes, who rounded Cape Horn eighty-four times, roamed the world's oceans during the nineteenth century as sealers, whalers, fishermen, and deepwater sailors. Their homes still cluster in the valley of the Mystic River.

Though the river is short, and the channel is narrow, it has floated the products of local shipyards since the 1780s. Over five hundred vessels were launched at Mystic from

47
Preceding pages: *The Seaport's Henry B. du Pont Preservation Shipyard in action. The* Sabino *sits on the lift dock for bottom work as the* Charles W. Morgan *is maneuvered into position to have her masts unrigged. Behind the* Sabino *is the main shop, large enough to accommodate the hull of the* Morgan, *if necessary. It houses the carpenter shop, a 97-foot spar lathe, a rigging loft, and a visitor observation gallery. As much as possible, the work is performed in view of the public.*

48
The restored figurehead of the Mystic-built ship Seminole *now guards the entrance to the Seaport's overview exhibit, ''New England and the Sea.''*

49 50

1784 to 1919, from fishing sloops to Civil War steamships to the clipper ship *Andrew Jackson*, which shares the record for the fastest sailing passage from New York to San Francisco with the legendary clipper *Flying Cloud*. From 1840 until the maritime decline following the Civil War, five or more Mystic shipyards hewed a steady stream of ships out of the area's timber. Mystic Seaport now encompasses the sites of two of those yards and much of Greenmanville, a shipyard and textile mill community associated with the George Greenman & Co. shipyard.

From the very beginning, Mystic Seaport has been more than a local marine museum. Early members donated paintings, models, scrimshaw, manuscripts, photographs, and other artifacts representing the full range of America's maritime endeavors. The fierce Indian figurehead of the ship *Seminole*, built at Mystic in 1865, often dove into the frigid swells off Cape Horn as Captain Holmes of Mystic drove his ship between New York and San Francisco. Among the museum's scrimshaw (carved whale ivory and baleen) are the exquisite domestic items carved by Captain Frederick H. Smith and his wife Sallie during their whaling voyages in the 1870s and '80s, which portray the gentle side of the characteristic New England whaling industry. Robert Weir's heavily illustrated journal of a whaling voyage is but one of the more than 1,000 ships' logbooks and journals that form the foundation of the museum's manuscript collection, housed in a modern library building. The Rosenfeld photograph collection contains over a million images and covers one hundred years of yachting history as witnessed by the famous maritime photographer Morris Rosenfeld, his talented family, and several earlier photographers. This recently purchased collection more than doubles in size the museum's broad collection of maritime images.

In addition to artifacts that could be contained in a traditional museum building, the three founders had vague dreams of building a waterfront community and exhibiting actual vessels. They considered a few dilapidated sailing vessels, such as the Down Easter

49
Frozen in the ice—and in time—the newly launched pilot schooner Telegram *lies off the Charles Mallory & Sons shipyard in December 1875. She was the last vessel built at the Mallory yard, one of ten shipyard locations active in Mystic between 1784 and 1919. This site is now partially occupied by the Seaport's restoration shipyard.*

50
"Sports of Whalemen," illustrating a hazard of the whaleman's life, is one of the exquisite sketches in Robert Weir's journal of his voyage in the whaleship Clara Bell, *1855–58.*

51
Rushing European emigrants to America, the Black Ball Line packet Neptune *charges through the New England fishing fleet anchored on the Grand Bank of Newfoundland. John E. C. Petersen painted this accurate scene in 1866.*

52
The "primitive" quality now admired in the work of some "pierhead" painters belies the accuracy of nautical detail they often achieved. The New York "clipper" schooner Carlos C. Colgate, *built at West Haven, Connecticut, in 1867, knifes through a fantastic sea in an 1869 watercolor by Jurgen Frederick Huge of Bridgeport, Connecticut.*

51

52

53

The iron-hulled, full-rigged ship Joseph Conrad *was built at Copenhagen in 1882 as the training ship* Georg Stage. *After fifty years of service preparing boys for the Danish sea services, she made a 'round-the-world voyage under Captain Alan Villiers in the mid-1930s. Further service as a yacht and as an American maritime training ship during World War II preceded her arrival at Mystic in 1947. At the Seaport the 111-foot* Conrad *is both an exhibit ship and the quarters for sail education programs.*

53

54   55

Benjamin F. Packard, but concluded that she was too large to reach the Association's location on the shallow Mystic River. Instead, they salvaged the *Packard*'s elegant after-cabin woodwork, which would be reassembled for exhibit thirty-five years later. Though the vessel is gone, visitors can still walk through the officers'quarters of this Cape Horn freighter of the 1880s.

The scope of Mystic's preservation effort expanded in 1941 when the plight of another vessel became known. The last surviving American sailing whaleship, the *Charles W. Morgan*, was in need of preservation. She had made thirty-seven whaling voyages during an eighty-year career, and at age one hundred had lost her sponsor as an exhibit ship. Carl Cutler, Mystic's moving force, accepted responsibility for her, bringing her to Mystic only weeks before the outbreak of World War II. Since then, visitors have flocked to Mystic to walk the deck and contemplate the dark, cramped quarters in the forecastle of the *Morgan*, which survived tropical storm, Arctic ice, and even a cannibal attack during her long service in the grisly but fascinating business memorialized in Herman Melville's *Moby-Dick*.

Following the war, the U.S. Government began to divest surplus elements of the war effort. One was the 1882 Danish training ship *Georg Stage*, which had been renamed *Joseph Conrad* when adventurer Alan Villiers purchased her for his 'round-the-world voyage in 1934. Seeking to carry through the dream of establishing a maritime training program, the Marine Historical Association applied for the *Conrad*, a request that was granted by an act of congress in 1947. A summer sailing program was created, which preserved the vessel, her original function, and basic maritime skills all in one stroke.

More recently, other significant vessels have been added to the Seaport's collection. New England's sea fisheries are represented by the classic fishing schooner *L. A. Dunton*. Built in 1921, the *Dunton* was among the last of her breed built to fish under sail alone, acting as mother ship to a fleet of dories from which her fishermen tugged cod,

54
The life of the deep-water sailor can be better comprehended after witnessing a sail-setting demonstration aboard the Joseph Conrad. *After unfurling the sail and letting it hang from its horizontal yard, the crew returns to the deck and hoists the yard with a block-and-tackle halyard.*

55
The 1908 steamboat Sabino, *one of the few surviving coal-fired passenger steamers in the U.S., gives visitors the rare experience of quiet steam propulsion as she cruises along the Seaport's waterfront.*

56

57

haddock, and halibut from the depths of the treacherous fishing grounds that stretch from Georges Bank to the Grand Bank of Newfoundland.

The revolutionary influence of marine steam power is reflected in the 1908 steamboat *Sabino*, which cruises noiselessly along the Seaport's waterfront, with only the jangle of bells to pass orders from captain to engineer and the shrill of her whistle to communicate with other vessels. Passengers can appreciate both the silent efficiency of a steam engine and the endless shoveling labor of the fireman, an overheated servant of the boiler's firebox.

The significance of small watercraft, from a Maine peapod still grimed with lobster bait to an exquisite sailing canoe gleaming in its golden varnish, is not lost among the Seaport's larger vessels. The museum has assembled the largest watercraft collection in an American museum, and probably in the world. At a working boatshop, replicas are built and, in the process, boatbuilding techniques are learned, revived, and preserved, and the performance and function of traditional boats can be studied and demonstrated.

As soon as it began to acquire real vessels, the museum renewed its plan to create a representative maritime community. The first building obtained was a shipsmith shop that once produced harpoons and ironwork for New Bedford's whaling fleet. Soon it was a familiar sight to see a barge bringing another forlorn building through the Mystic River bascule bridge on its way to the museum grounds. The community area soon took a direction of its own, as the museum assembled a picturesque village on the long abandoned site of the Greenman shipyard.

In its outdoor exhibits, the Seaport concentrates on the New England coast during the century of change, 1814–1914, which saw the American merchant marine reach its height and then change completely in the face of technological progress. Buildings collected by the museum represent this theme. A U.S. Life-Saving Service station built on Block Island, Rhode Island, in 1874 demonstrates increasing concern over the hazards of

56
Among the many buildings to arrive at the Seaport by barge was the Thomas Oyster Co. building, shown here en route from New Haven to Mystic in 1972.

57
A winter still life captures a wind-sculpted drift and lobster pots at the lobstering exhibit. Frozen in the background are the Thomas Oyster Co. building and the oyster dredging sloop Nellie.

58
The Charles Mallory Sail Loft and the Plymouth Cordage Co. ropewalk exhibit represent essential maritime trades of a seaport community. The sail loft building houses a chandlery exhibit and a rigging loft on its lower floors.

sea travel, which eventually resulted in the U.S. Coast Guard. An essential maritime industry of the age of sail is represented by the Mallory Sail Loft, owned by a Mystic entrepreneur who worked his way from sailmaker to steamship operator.

Indicative of a fishery that changed little during the century is the Ames Fish House, which stands on the beach, much as it did on the shore of Penobscot Bay, Maine, waiting for its owner to set his pound net and entrap Atlantic salmon on their spring migration up the Penobscot River. Nearby, the Thomas Thomas Oyster House from New Haven, Connecticut, once again sits upon a wharf with an oyster-dredging sloop tied alongside as if to unload its briny cargo for sorting and shipment to a hungry market. Thomas Thomas was a leader in the pioneering mariculture of the Connecticut oyster industry.

Some acquired buildings have both maritime and architectural significance, such as the New York Yacht Club's original clubhouse. This picturesque gothic structure, built at Hoboken, New Jersey, in 1845, was probably designed by the noted architect Andrew Jackson Davis. It suggests the increasing importance of the recreational uses of the sea. Some buildings have limited maritime connections, but were important structures, such as the classical stone Mystic Bank building of 1833, or the 1768 Samuel Buckingham House, plucked from the path of highway construction near the Connecticut River. Now the broad hearth of the Buckingham House blazes anew in demonstrations of early nineteenth-century coastal cooking.

Artifacts, ships, and buildings are the most obvious elements of maritime preservation at Mystic Seaport, but there is another dimension as well. It takes human contact to bring us back in touch with our maritime past and elucidate the intangible human element. Maritime crafts, such as shipsmithing, ship carving, and coopering have been demonstrated by exhibit interpreters for many years. In addition, outdoor demonstrations have become some of the most effective methods of preserving maritime skills. Accurate

59

59
The Victorian elegance of the captain's day cabin, with its etched glass, gold leafing, and rich veneered woods, is part of the painstaking restoration of the after cabin of the Benjamin F. Packard. *The 244-foot sailing cargo carrier was built in 1883 to haul California grain around Cape Horn.*

60

The Gothic Revival design of the New York Yacht Club's 1845 original clubhouse is attributed to the noted architect Andrew Jackson Davis. The restoration's color scheme has been authenticated to an early period of the building's use. In the background is the cupola of the Seaport's G. W. Blunt White Library.

61

The skilled hands of the caulker drive strands of oakum (tarred hemp) into the seams between the Morgan's planking.

62

In the James Driggs Shipsmith Shop of 1885, an interpreter demonstrates the forging of iron into nautical implements.

60

61

62

demonstrations of such activities as sail setting and furling, whaleboat use, fish processing, and a breeches buoy rescue drill not only preserve the essence of these maritime skills, they also communicate nuances of past maritime experiences. Sea music was also integral to maritime life. Music as an expression of emotion, music as a tool to coordinate work, music as a participatory amusement: all of these elements are recalled during the musical activities at the Seaport.

Roleplaying takes a final step toward preserving and communicating the most personal aspects of maritime history. A few interpreters have studied diaries, letters, and other personal expressions of nineteenth-century individuals to the point where they can step into character and talk as wives worried about their husbands at sea, as sailors ashore between voyages, as widows concerned about sailors' welfare, or as maritime businessmen. During the Seaport's Christmas Lantern Light Tours, roleplayers portray the holiday's maritime incarnations as they changed through the nineteenth century. Each of these approaches is meant to restore the human element to the artifacts on view.

But among all of its programs, the one that most visibly symbolizes Mystic Seaport's commitment to maritime preservation is its fully equipped and professionally staffed shipyard. Its vessels most clearly distinguish Mystic Seaport from other maritime museums, and its shipyard is a model establishment for the maintenance of those vessels. Wooden, and even iron, ships require constant care. Yet, not until the 1960s were the overwhelming needs of those vessels fully recognized. Completed in the early 1970s, the Henry B. duPont Preservation Shipyard was designed to allow the museum to accomplish nearly all of its own vessel work. The shipyard's lift dock has the capacity to lift any of the museum's vessels clear of the water for major structural work, and the spar lathe can turn any mast, yard, or boom that might be necessary. From the sawmill to the rigging loft to the ironworking shop, the shipyard incorporates all of the traditional shipbuilding skills. Using the proper woods, wielding traditional hand tools whenever warranted, and carrying out the work to allow visitors to see the intricacies of shipbuilding, the shipwrights are both craftsmen who preserve artifacts and perpetuate skills and teachers who demonstrate those skills.

Mystic Seaport is widely known for its ships and its excellent collection of small craft, its buildings, working exhibits, and other evidence of New England's varied ties with the sea, its photographic collections, and for its library and associated graduate and undergraduate programs in maritime studies. While these elements are at the heart of the museum, the lifeblood of the Seaport is its people: members, volunteers, and staff with a common commitment to the preservation of our maritime heritage.

63
Mystic Seaport Museum incorporates elements of a 19th-century working waterfront. Here, the pinky Regina M. *is docked near the Mystic Bank and the cooperage exhibit.*

63

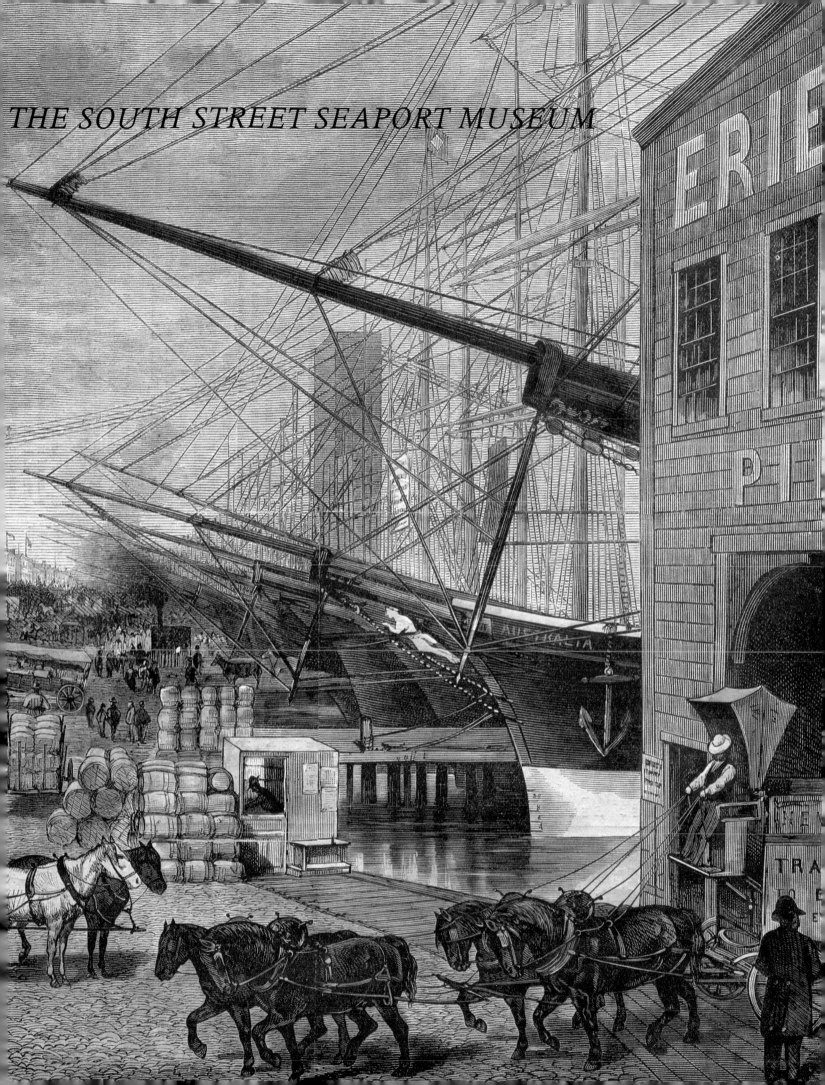

4 The Street of Ships:
Immigration and International Commerce in New York

Peter Neill, President

The South Street Seaport Museum

NEW YORK

With the arrival of the Dutch in the 1620s, the harbor of New Amsterdam, later New York, began a rise to preeminence that continues to this day. An estuarine confluence of rivers and the sea, sheltered and strategically located, the Port of New York evinced, indeed frequently determined, important aspects of our nation's history and the development of its commerce and culture. New York served as the threshold of America for countless immigrants, as a major port for transoceanic, coastal, and interior trade, and as a national center for finance, technology, and the arts. New York was the destination of the first regularly scheduled packet ships from Liverpool, England, and the continental ports. New York was the center of a coasting trade that distributed imports and assembled exports—to and from New England, the southern states, and the islands. New York was the terminus of an elaborate canal system, that remarkable early nineteenth-century engineering feat that opened the interior of our young nation to the world. New York was the port of embarkation for the great clipper ships that dared Cape Horn en route to California, China, and Japan. The center of all this maritime activity was the street that served the East River docks of Manhattan: the tangle of masts, yards, rigging, bowsprits angled toward the brick facades of mercantile buildings, cargo from Europe and Asia, loading, off-loading, transporting, selling, the shouts of merchants, bosuns, draymen, stevedores, buskers, thieves, the polyglot of language, the flux and influx of things, people, ideas: South Street, the street of ships.

This exuberance fired related activity, a concentric expansion of derivative enterprise. The intersecting streets were lined with countinghouses, warehouses, and the banking, insurance, and printing businesses that served this commerce on Water Street, Wall Street, and Maiden Lane. The cloth merchants, and then the first fashion houses, lined Pearl Street. Sailmakers, coopers, and shipwrights plied their trades; shipyards flourished on Peck's Slip and Dover Street. The Washington and Fulton markets were

64
Preceding pages: *View of South Street, New York ca. 1875, clogged with drays, wagons, horses, and people from all walks of life. The newly constructed Manhattan tower of the Brooklyn Bridge looms in the distance, nearly obscured by the tangle of masts and rigging.*

65
Masts of South Street sailing ships reaching skyward create a striking silhouette in this ca. 1900 photograph.

66

68

67

66
*Ferries and commuter steamboats,
leave from Peck's Slip. In the
background are the jam-packed East
River piers. This 1880s photograph
was taken from the Manhattan tower
of the Brooklyn Bridge.*

67
*The interior of the original 1821
Fulton Market, seen here in the late
1860s, housed all types of
merchants—from fishmongers to
booksellers. There were three
subsequent markets built on the site at
Fulton and Front streets. The last was
completed in 1983 as part of the
Seaport District revitalization.*

68
*The Fulton Ferry terminal, built in
the 1860s at South and Fulton streets,
was used until ferry service was
discontinued in 1924. Ferries linked
Manhattan's Fulton Street with
Fulton Street in Brooklyn.*

founded for the distribution of produce and fish. Ferryboats linked Fulton Street to the corresponding development of Fulton Street in Brooklyn. An extraordinary system of waterborne transport delivered everything from fresh water to waste, building materials, food; a concomitant system of quarters, rich and poor, hotels, seamen's homes, watering holes, restaurants, brothels, and floating churches served equally utilitarian needs. All the fundamentals and all the frivolities of a burgeoning nineteenth-century metropolis were evident.

So, too, was rapid technological change. At mid-century, the great age of sail began its decline, supplanted by steam-powered vessels and, more importantly, by the railroads. While South Street still saw sailing vessels well into the twentieth century, the number

69

was sadly diminished. The piers on the Hudson River side of Manhattan began to receive the deeper draft steamships, freighters, and ocean liners, these larger vessels requiring substantial construction and repair service. The Brooklyn Navy Yard and the yards of Erie Basin, Staten Island, and New Jersey emerged; hundreds of new docks were built in the bays, canals, and creeks of the five boroughs. Most everything still moved by water, by tugs and barges, floating grain elevators, and by an enormous fleet of lighters and car ferries to facilitate the requirements of trans-shipment to rail. This spreading economic vitality transcended South Street and, slowly, inevitably, as the industrial potential of the region was realized, what had been exclusively an East River phenomenon grew to become the complex collective known as the Port of New York.

69
A bird's eye view of Manhattan in 1876, by Currier and Ives, shows the variety of vessels at work in New York Harbor in the last half of the 19th century.

71   72

But the true significance of South Street lies beyond its history as the physical location of early maritime trade. As important is the correlation between such activity and the social development of the city, the evolution of community, class, and culture. The impact of successive waves of immigration, for example, formed New York's diverse ethnic personality, its confusion of language, religion, and neighborhood, its contradiction of politics. The maritime trades were early to react against the adverse effects of population growth and rapid change—the dockworkers, for example, founding the first unions to protect their employment and wages. Artisans, their skills obsolete in an industrializing world, became managers, clerks, or laborers, creating inevitable distinctions of finance and class. Countinghouses became banks, warehouses became brokerages, captains became merchants and merchants became millionaires. There was unconscionable exploitation—of slaves, children, women, minorities, the poor. Of course, the social revolution that swept nineteenth-century America is far more complicated than this, nor was it unique to New York. But the city was the focus of much of the innovation, execution, abuse, and reform that constitutes a remarkable history, a fascinating narrative—and South Street figures in almost every theme and aspect.

In 1968, the South Street Seaport Museum was founded to collect, preserve, and interpret the artifacts and skills which document the maritime contribution to the history of culture and commerce of the City of New York, the state, and the nation. Indeed, the

70
The masts and yards of the Peking, *the museum's 1911 four-masted bark, rise above the chimneys of the restored Schermerhorn Row buildings.*

71
Bowne & Co., Stationers, is the museum's recreation of an 1870s printer's and stationer's shop. It is typical of those that flourished in downtown New York, serving the mercantile and shipping community. Inside, visitors can watch skilled artisans carry out letterpress printing.

72
Schermerhorn Row, restored in 1983 and today occupied by retail businesses, reflects South Street's countinghouse days and heralds the district's commercial revival.

purpose is international in scope, New York being the connection—across the seas and via ships—with the peoples and customs that created our way of life.

The museum's greatest artifact, then, is the port itself, from the backwaters of Newtown Creek, the Morris Canal, and the Kill Van Kull to the sprawling container facilities of Port Newark and Port Elizabeth. While today the maritime industry is generally depressed worldwide, New York still handles more cargo tonnage than any other port. The harbor reaches are crowded still with Staten Island ferryboats, tugs, garbage scows, oil barges, tankers, freighters, U.S. Coast Guard vessels, New York City police and fireboats. Recently, commuter ferries have returned to connect Manhattan with New Jersey, and the excursion business has been revitalized, including the museum-sponsored Seaport Line which operates the *Andrew Fletcher* and the *DeWitt Clinton*, replicas of representative nineteenth-century tour boats.

New York, like the rest of America, is rediscovering the waterfront that it abandoned with the decline of maritime activity and that was cut off from the city center by rail lines, superhighways, and dilapidated piers. Dockage was nearly nonexistent in New York until recently, and, in 1986, when the museum opened a modest facility on Pier 15 for transient boats, it was an immediate success. So, too, with recreational boating, once an exciting aspect of a harbor that hosted the America's Cup challenges for more than fifty years. At the turn of the century, "sandbagger" regattas were a familiar sight on New York waters, wonderful sloops that on weekends were transformed from workboats into racing machines manned by crews from the local bars. No rules, no protests, sandbags for ballast and carry all the sail you like, drunk or sober; it was competition of a most beautiful and cutthroat kind. The museum owns *Shadow*, one of the few remaining sandbaggers, which it intends to replicate for syndicates wishing to restore this colorful racing to the harbor.

A most exhilarating expression of this maritime renaissance was the Operation Sail contribution to the 1986 Statue of Liberty Centennial. The "tall ships" of 23 nations led a parade witnessed by a spectator fleet estimated at more than 40,000 vessels and by a television audience of millions. Fifteen historic ships docked at the museum; some 350,000 people visited the piers over three days, and 42,000 were boarded for tours. If ever South Street was to be again the "street of ships," that was the moment, and the museum, devoted to evocation of the past, was able to demonstrate, indeed celebrate, that heritage in the present.

Many maritime museums have made the decision not to keep ships, and there is ample reason, primarily the high cost. Nevertheless, the grandeur of the ships is unquestionable; like cathedrals, they have beauty and scale; like dinosaurs, they have mystery. Moreover, the ships are inextricably linked to tales of exploration, adventure, and survival, of self-reliance, cooperation, and competence. The ships inspire; they provoke understanding of values diminished in our modern time, behavior well worth preserving.

73
Operation Sail 1986 brought renewed maritime activity to New York Harbor. Among the vessels docked at museum piers was the U.S. Coast Guard's Eagle, *shown here dressed with flags from bow to stern. In the foreground is the* Ambrose, *the museum's 1908 lightship.*

74

Thus, while the decision not to keep ships may be incontrovertibly practical, it confounds the romance and denies the power of these, the most threatened reality and symbol of our maritime tradition.

The South Street Seaport Museum keeps one of the most significant fleets of historic vessels in the world. Foremost among them is the great four-masted bark *Peking*, at 347 feet one of the largest sailing vessels still afloat. Built in Germany in 1911, *Peking* was fast and efficient, carrying more than an acre of sail and manned by only 28 men. Throughout her career, she transported general cargo to the west coast of South America, and returned with nitrates to fertilize the fields of Europe. In 1931, she was retired to become a schoolship in England; in 1974, she was purchased for South Street and towed to New York where she is being rerigged and her captain's cabin, mates' staterooms, seamen's foc'sle, and sail room restored.

The British full-rigged ship *Wavertree* was built in Southampton in 1885 just as steel was replacing wrought iron as ship-building material. A workhorse of ocean trade, she is the last remaining of over 3,000 similar vessels to have been constructed. *Wavertree* was a "tramper," taking whatever paying cargo she could find; grain from Australia, lumber from Oregon, coal from Europe. In 1895, she called at South Street with South American nitrate, and departed with kerosene for Calcutta. In 1910, she was dismasted off Cape Horn, limped into the Falkland Islands, and was sold as a floating warehouse in the Straits

74
The museum's sidewheeler Andrew Fletcher, *a replica of vessels that plied East River waters a century ago, leaves her Pier 17 berth on one of her daily tours of New York Harbor.*

75
A winter night scene of the Peking *berthed beneath the monolithic towers of downtown Manhattan.*

75

of Magellan. After 37 years in such service, she was towed to Buenos Aires where, in 1966, she was discovered, a sand barge in a backwater of the Riachuelo River, her iron plating still in excellent condition. She was brought to New York in 1970 where her restoration is continuing, perhaps even to sail again.

The museum's other ships include *Ambrose* (1908), a lightship that for two decades lit the way for ships through Ambrose Channel into the port of New York; *Pioneer* (1885), a coasting cargo schooner built for the Delaware River that the museum operates under sail for educational programs; *Lettie G. Howard* (1893), the last of the Fredonia inshore fishing schooners that called by the hundreds with fish for Fulton Market; *Major General*

76
South Street piers evoked an earlier era with a tangle of masts during Operation Sail 1986. Docked at the museum piers were the Eagle, *the restored* Elissa *from Galveston, Texas, and the Mexican training ship* Cuauhtemoc, *strung with lights for the festivities. They were among 15 historic ships docked at the museum.*

77

Wm. H. Hart (1925), a steam-powered New York ferryboat, and *W. O. Decker* (1930), the last wood-constructed tugboat to work the harbor.

In addition, South Street is the keeper of a remarkable collection of buildings, in effect, "a museum without walls." In 1978, the City of New York transferred to the museum a 99-year lease for the five-block historic district between Peck's and Burling slips, an area characterized by its varied and distinguished architecture. Subsequently, the museum, in joint venture with the state, city, and the Rouse Company of Columbia, Md., rebuilt Piers 16 and 17 and rehabilitated numerous landmark buildings on Fulton, Water, Front, and John streets. Primary among these are Schermerhorn Row, built in 1812, and

77
Schooners vie for the start in the annual Mayor's Cup Schooner Race sponsored by the museum for the past 21 years. The race in New York Harbor hosts dozens of schooners, once common work boats in the waters surrounding Manhattan.

78

79

the A.A. Low building, a splendid example of a substantial brownstone countinghouse built in 1850 for New York's premier China trade merchant.

Since 1726, the Schermerhorn family had been active in purchasing parcels of New York real estate. In 1811, Peter Schermerhorn (1749–1826) consolidated the family's holdings in the area, both land and ''water-lots,'' semi-submerged properties that were buildable only if filled by dumped refuse. Almost all of the shoreline of contemporary lower Manhattan is nineteenth-century landfill, and present-day developers continue to follow this precedent, proposing remarkably similar construction projects. Much of the

78
This tranquil view from the forecastle head of the Peking *across the slip to the* Wavertree, *the museum's 1885 full-rigged ship, belies the treacherous ocean voyages endured by both vessels.*

79
The W. O. Decker, the last wood-constructed tugboat to work in New York Harbor, is tied to the Ambrose on a snowy winter morning. Both vessels are in the museum's collection.

museum's important collection of archaeological materials has been excavated from such sites recently disturbed for the construction of modern office towers. The upper floors of the Row are presently being renovated to contain the museum's new permanent exhibit on the history of the Port of New York.

If Schermerhorn was the typical real estate speculator, then A. A. Low and his brothers were the typical merchant bankers. The clipper ship was America's great contribution to marine technology, these sleek sailing craft shrinking the world with their record-breaking transoceanic passages. A fleet of these vessels was built for the Lows, including the *Montauk*, the *Samuel Russell*, the *Surprise*, the *Oriental*, and the *Great Republic*. These were the ships that established the far-eastern trade, importing tea, silks, and porcelains from China and Japan. One of these ships, the *Hoqua*, was named for the Chinese hong merchant who had schooled Abiel Abbot Low in the lessons of doing business in Canton. The Low Building was completed in 1850; today, its original cast-iron facade still intact, it houses the museum's collections and changing exhibition galleries.

While the museum offers a variety of programs in four additional spaces, it shares the district with retail stores, numerous restaurants, and the Fulton Fish Market. This partnership has been somewhat controversial, some critics arguing that it is "too commercial." As South Street was always commercial, clustering wholesalers, retailers, and purveyors of food and drink in its bustling neighborhood, this criticism is perhaps informed more by nostalgia than by history. Suffice it to say that the redevelopment of the district has preserved the buildings, created an audience of tourist and city dweller alike, and generated major financial support for the museum.

In 1836, Samuel Griswold Goodrich published *Peter Parley's Visit to New York*, a charming account of a visit to a city which, by that time, had become one of the world's great centers of enterprise and civilization. The hero, young Peter Parley, immerses himself in city life and exults over all he sees. In his enthusiasm, he proclaims a chauvinistic sentiment that may still pertain: "The sun, as it passes round the earth, shines upon no ocean where it does not also shine upon the white sails of ships that are steering their way to New York."

To South Street, the street of ships.

80
The Brooklyn Bridge—that monumental feat of human engineering and daring—rises from the mist in this photograph. The bridge remains a symbol of the challenge and achievement of New York.

THE THOUSAND ISLANDS SHIPYARD MUSEUM

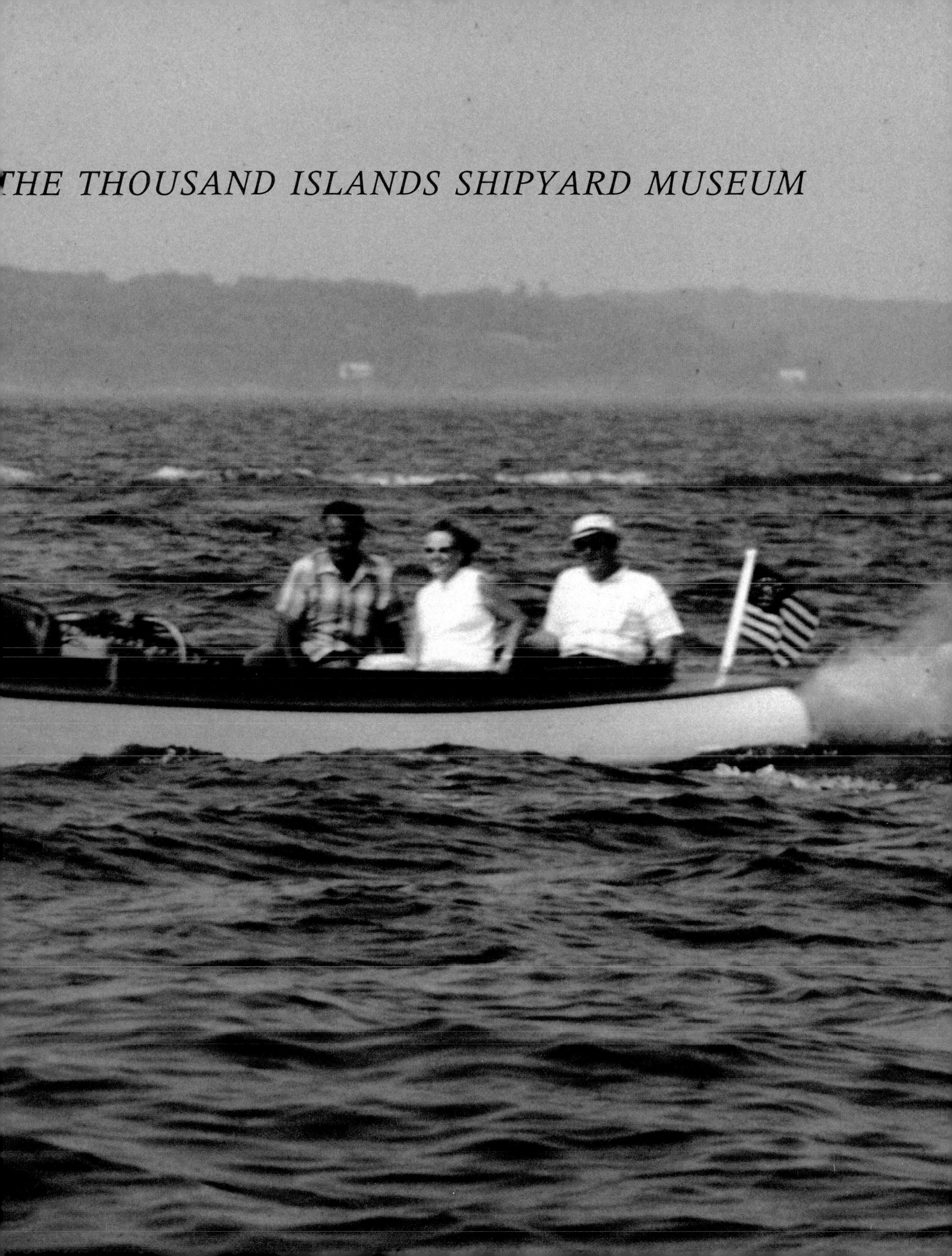

82

83

84

85

86

87

88

5 Gold Cup Racing, Rumrunning, and the Lore of the St. Lawrence River
Laurie Watson Rush, Assistant Director, and Dawn E. Rusho, Research Associate

The Thousand Islands Shipyard Museum

CLAYTON · NEW YORK

Dazzling racing boats that feed man's desire for recreation and competition; silent non-power craft that allow him to be one with nature; sporty runabouts designed for family transportation and fun; punts propelled across the ice by airplane engines; a dugout canoe buried in a river bank for a hundred years; all of these are part of our freshwater nautical history. The Thousand Islands Shipyard Museum in Clayton, New York, is dedicated to preserving this heritage of the St. Lawrence River and her boats. Located on the banks of the St. Lawrence River in northern New York State, the museum boasts one of the country's finest collections of antique, freshwater small craft.

From the air, in the summer, the Thousand Islands look like green jewels, set against a background of rich blue fabric. On closer inspection, it is clear that each island is its own vacation paradise. The water is dotted with pleasure craft of all shapes and sizes, many with colorful sails or sleek wood finishes. A huge oceangoing vessel or Great Lakes freighter occasionally interrupts the scene as it plies the route down the St. Lawrence Seaway.

In prehistoric times, a view of the islands would have revealed Indian villages and camps with people fishing, hunting, and setting weirs for eels. The water would have been dotted with dugouts and bark canoes of various sizes. The river, then as now, was a major highway for commerce, trade, migration, and warfare.

In silent testimony to less peaceful times, chimneys stand on the bluffs of Carleton Island. They are the last visible remains of Fort Haldimand, a base for British raids on northern New York during the American Revolution. Fort Haldimand was already crumbling when an American commander brought his expeditionary force up the St. Lawrence to fight the British in the War of 1812. He camped not far from the Shipyard Museum grounds in the seclusion of French Creek. American outlaws tried one last time to stir up

81

Preceding pages: *The first and original* PDQ, *built in 1904 in Ogdensburg, New York, makes an appearance on the St. Lawrence River. There were six* PDQ's *built for and raced by members of the Boldt family. The original* PDQ *was 37 feet long, with a 4-foot 9-inch beam. Driving* PDQ IV *47 m.p.h., Louise Clover Miles took the fastest motorboat time made by a woman up to that time, winning from her husband in* PDQ V.

*Around the turn of the century, the summer social life in the Thousand Islands area rivaled Newport's. Presidents vacationed here, millionaires built castles for summer homes, elegant steam yachts were frequent sights on the river, and several trains a day unloaded their carloads of passengers at docks in Clayton and Alexandria Bay.—82— Steamboat passengers boarding from the wharf of the Frontenac Hotel— 83—Romantic Boldt Castle, built on Heart Island at the turn of the century for George Boldt of the Waldorf Astoria—84—President Chester Arthur during a Thousand Islands fishing trip aboard a St. Lawrence River skiff—85—Looking to catch a big one from a St. Lawrence skiff along the rocky island shoreline— 86—*Dixie II, *winner of 106 out of 107 races—87—Hopewell Hall, a luxurious Victorian island summer home on the St. Lawrence River— 88—The Frontenac Hotel, the ultimate island vacation resort*

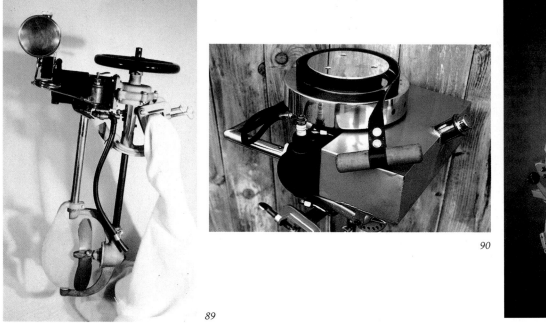

89

90

91

hostility toward the British in the Patriot's War of 1838 and stories about Pirate Bill Johnston, a figure in this activity, still abound.

Today ruins and restorations of fortifications along the shorelines can be explored by the curious traveler and history buff alike. In contrast to the past's warships filled with conscripts, these monuments now watch over people enjoying the water; fishing, sailing, waterskiing, parasailing, and racing.

When the border became peaceful, the waterways quickly filled with schooners and steamers carrying freight and trading throughout the lakes and rivers. Millions of feet of lumber were built into timber rafts of immense proportions which were disassembled to shoot the rapids on their way to British timber markets downsteam.

During this prosperity, it took no time at all for the American leisure class to discover the vacation possibilities of the Thousand Islands. It was a fabulous era of palatial summer homes and luxurious hotels. As many as five trains a day brought visitors to Clayton from New York City alone, and ferries and steamers met them at the railroad docks to take them to their island and Canadian destinations.

Thousand Islands Park with its spectacular array of gingerbread summer homes was built, and exclusive summer home communities like the Round Island Association were established. Presidents came to vacation, and castles were built for summer homes. Elegant hotels like the Frontenac, Thousand Islands House, and the Crossmon House were built to accommodate the growing number of visitors. Just growing fresh flowers for the hotel tables was a full-time enterprise.

The wealthy visitors enjoyed all types of island diversions: polo, nighttime

89
A 1912, 2-hp Waterman outboard engine. The engine was started by giving the heavy flywheel a vigorous turn. Waterman was the first financially successful American outboard maker.

90
The first Johnson outboard ever made, built in 1921. This outboard was personally presented to the museum by Warren Conover, brother-in-law of the Johnsons and cofounder of the corporation.

91
Scott/McCulloch diesel outboard engine, ca. 1963. Only twenty-one of these 150-hp, 2-stroke engines were made.

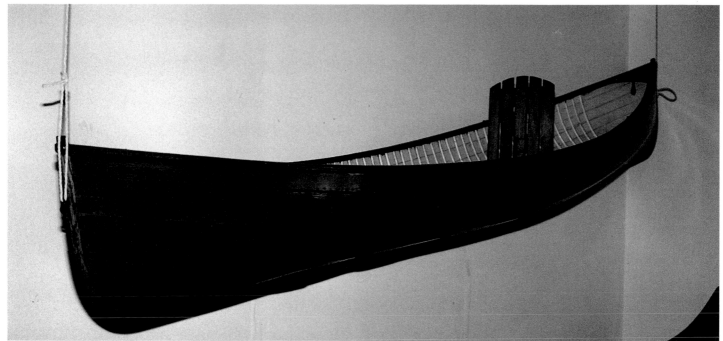

92

searchlight cruises, shore dinners, and, of course, boat racing. Racing on the water was a natural pastime for the wealthy summer residents, and it was not unusual to see large steam yachts competing for a ''winner's purse'' or in match races. With the advent of gasoline engines, attention turned to smaller boats, and the Chippewa Bay Yacht Club's entry *Chip I* brought the Gold Cup competition to the Thousand Islands by winning the second Gold Cup race on the Hudson River in 1905. In their efforts to outdo each other, yacht club members produced vessels like *Dixie II* and *PDQ*. Winning the Gold Cup offers the privilege of hosting the race, and so the Gold Cup Races were held on the St. Lawrence during those days of glory, from 1905–13. At that time, *Ankle Deep* won the race for the Lake George Regatta Association, taking the Gold Cup away from the river, never to return.

Often referred to as the Grande Dame of Gold Cup racing, *Dixie II* was the winner of three Gold Cups and two Harmsworth International Trophies. She won 106 of 107 races and held the speed record, set in 1910, for displacement hulls of twelve meters, of 45 miles per hour. Ironically, no sooner had she achieved this record than she was retired, having been rendered obsolete by the development of hydroplane hulls.

PDQ II, a Gold Cup racer from 1904, is also part of the Shipyard Museum's extensive boat collection. Her owner was George Boldt, owner-manager of the Bellevue Stratford and manager of the KW Waldorf Astoria hotels, builder of Boldt Castle on Heart Island, and owner of a fleet of eighteen vessels including a sailing yacht, several steam yachts, a number of motorboats, and a 105-foot double-decker houseboat, *La Duchesse.*

The 1920s ushered excitement of a different sort into the islands: bootlegging. The

92
An 18-pound ''Nessmuk Canoe'' built by John Henry Rushton, ca. 1881–82. Rushton, of Canton, New York, was known for his strong, yet lightweight canoes.

Canadian boundary, established along a waterway filled with natural promontories for lookouts, coves, bays, and channels for hiding places, as well as resourceful independent citizens, made the area ideal for smuggling. During Prohibition, liquor came through the islands by horse, handsled, sailboat, power boat, ferry boat, skiff, ice punt, and airplane. Smugglers drove, walked, sailed, and rowed, hiding liquor in everything from burlap sacks to wild animal cages, milk cans, and dead fish.

In spite of the few dedicated agents, efforts to stop the smuggling were often fruitless, with telephone operators even tipping off the bootleggers. Some local citizens still remember high-speed chases over country roads and gunshots in the night.

The desire to elude the Coast Guard encouraged local builders to design small streamlined boats with powerful engines, and the post-Prohibition speedster *Misbehave*, typical of this type of boat, is a popular exhibit at the museum.

But the small craft heritage of the St. Lawrence is much more than just fast boats. Before the evolution of gasoline motors, the St. Lawrence skiff was developed in the Thousand Islands as a fishing guide's boat, used both for rowing and sailing. This skiff is renowned for its graceful lines, ease of handling, durability, and the fact that, uniquely, it can be and is sailed without the aid of a rudder. At the turn of the century, families summering in the Thousand Islands often relied on the skiff for transporting guests, doing the marketing, and, of course, fishing. Photographs document President Ulysses S. Grant's and President Chester A. Arthur's use and enjoyment of this craft when they visited the area. Eventually, due to a local spirit of friendly competition among skiff owners, both rowing and sailing races developed, still popular yearly events held on the river. Even later, as faster means of propulsion were developed, the skiff was adapted to accommodate the marine engine and evolved into the skiff putt and "Stump-Jumper," or disappearing propeller boat.

Rushton canoes form another significant element of the North Country boatbuilding tradition. John Henry Rushton made his name building lightweight yet durable and stable rowboats and canoes in Canton, N. Y., at the turn of the century. His customers included artist Frederic Remington and author G. W. Sears, who wrote under the pen name Nessmuk. Sears, who traveled Adirondack lakes often and alone, commissioned Rushton to build a canoe weighing less than 20 pounds and yet capable of carrying 150 pounds. The final product, on display at the Adirondack Museum, actually weighed less than 18 pounds.

The history of freshwater boating is incomplete without mention of marine engines—the power behind the hulls. In the early 1900s, the industrial revolution brought huge technological advances to maritime design as to every other aspect of transportation. With the advent of steam and then the gasoline-powered motor, unheard-of speed could be achieved. Mass production eventually made the building of these newly

93
A river craft unique to the St. Lawrence River, the ice punt is propelled by an airplane engine and is able to travel on ice or through water. In fall and spring, the ice punt is often the only means for reaching island homes.

94
Entrance to the Thousand Islands Shipyard Museum in Clayton, N.Y.

95
1908–10 Gold Cup winner, Dixie II *impresses the audience at a recent Antique Boat Show. Known to some as "Queen of the Gold Cup Racers,"* Dixie II *won three Gold Cups and two Harmsworth Trophies. She still holds the world speed record for boats with displacement hulls.*

93

94

95

96

96
*Still operational, the classic launch
Anita runs on naphtha fuel. She was
built in 1902 and in 1985 was
honored as Queen of the 75th Annual
New York Boat Show.*

97   98

designed boats and motors available to a wide population. The move to automation during those years increased available leisure time, and, combined with newfound wealth, provided not only the money to buy boats but also the time to enjoy cruising in them.

The Thousand Islands Shipyard Museum dramatically documents the history of power boating. Included in its collections are more than 130 outboards and 60 inboards, spanning the development of marine propulsion systems from the late 1800s to post–World War II times.

The collection also includes the oldest known outboard in existence, the French motogodille, circa 1904, and the first Johnson outboard ever manufactured. There are also examples of boats developed by such companies as Chris-Craft, Garwood, Hacker, Lyman, and Century as well as finely crafted boats from local builders such as the Hutchinson Boat Works of Alexandria Bay, New York.

The museum has just added the spectacular 48-foot custom runabout *Pardon Me* to its collection. This boat, designed by John Hacker in 1947 and powered by an 1,800-horsepower Packard engine, was considered by many to be Hutchinson's finest work.

Because of the St. Lawrence River tradition of fine small craft, river residents became the first in North America to inaugurate an Antique Boat Show in 1964. The enthusiasm generated by the show expanded into an antique boat auxiliary for the local town history museum. In 1971 the boat museum moved to a permanent location, steadily

97, 98
Spectators admire antique launches during an Antique Boat Show. Canopied launches, popular at the turn of the century, were ideal for relaxed Sunday afternoon outings and picnics.

expanded, and formally became the Thousand Islands Shipyard Museum in 1980. The museum occupies eight buildings today on 2.5 acres along the edge of a large bay on a picturesque harbor. A landscaped garden, a deck, and a delightful waterfront picnic area add to the visitor's enjoyment when visiting the museum's galleries and exhibitions.

The Antique Boat Show in Clayton is an annual event on the first full weekend of August each year, drawing 175 competitors and over 5,000 spectators to see competition in categories such as production launches, fishing guide boats, racing craft, canoes, skiffs, inboard motors, and outboard engines. Entries frequently include every type of craft from canoes to tall ships. Outboards that have stood the test of time must run for all to see. Often the high point of the show is an antique boat parade where exhibitors display their boats in an on-the-water procession, St. Lawrence River style.

Beyond hosting a boat show, however, the Shipyard Museum's mission is to preserve freshwater nautical history and tradition. Regional American prehistory is represented by dugout and birchbark canoes, and there are examples of the famous Adirondack guideboat. Besides the many outboard and inboard motors and racing craft displayed, there are tiny but speedy hydroplanes. In contrast to racing craft, launches and elegant small craft intended for recreation only, functional launches, caretaker boats, commercial craft, tour boats, ferries, steamers, punts, and fishing boats reflect another side of maritime activity. Treasures such as "Skinner Spoon" fishing lures, remnants of the steamer *Nightingale*, engravings of Bartlett's paintings along the St. Lawrence circa 1840, and an 1836 survey chart of Lake Ontario help to round out the exhibitions.

Indeed, the lore of the St. Lawrence River and freshwater small craft of all kinds from both past and present are celebrated eloquently by the collections of the Thousand Islands Shipyard Museum.

99

THE PHILADELPHIA MARITIME MUSEUM

6 *The Delaware River—America's Clyde*
Philip Chadwick Foster Smith,
Museum Historian and Former Curator

The Philadelphia Maritime Museum

PHILADELPHIA · PENNSYLVANIA

From source to mouth, the Delaware River twists and turns for 390 miles. It is roughly equivalent in length to the Connecticut, the Illinois, the Potomac, the Roanoke, and the Sacramento rivers. It is longer than the Hudson, the Kentucky, the Savannah, and the Tallahatchie, but it is only one-sixth the flow of the Mississippi. In sheer size it is not immense, yet in shipping enterprise and tradition the Delaware holds its own against the best of other navigable rivers.

Today, many people don't even think of Philadelphia as a port. Comparisons are therefore helpful to banish obstinate mists from the mind.

Central Philadelphia is situated just above the confluence of the Schuylkill (pronounced *school-kill*) and Delaware rivers, approximately one hundred miles up on the Delaware Bay and River from capes May and Henlopen and, hence, the Atlantic Ocean. The port of Canton (Guangzhou) in China lies about the same distance up the Pearl River above the South China Sea, as does the port of Buenos Aires on the Rio de la Plata in Argentina.

Similarly, New Orleans, the most active seaport in the United States and the second busiest in the world, after Rotterdam, lies as far up the Mississippi River from the Head of Passes into the Gulf of Mexico as does Philadelphia from the capes. Deep-water trade, furthermore, terminates at neither New Orleans nor Philadelphia. The head of navigation for ocean-borne commerce on the Mississippi is at Baton Rouge, 130 miles farther up; the equivalent in the Delaware River is Trenton, New Jersey, approximately thirty miles above the City of Brotherly Love.

To some people, the realization that huge blue-water vessels routinely venture so far up rivers from open seas comes as a genuine surprise. Even many native Philadelphians rarely think of their city as a port of any significance, international or otherwise. For outsiders, conventional mental images of Independence Hall, Betsy Ross, Benjamin

100
Preceding pages: *"Sectional Floating Dry Dock, J. Simpson & Neill Ship Wrights & Proprietors,"* chromolithograph by William Rease and F.H. Schell of Philadelphia, ca. 1860. The dock was at the foot of Christian Street in the Southwark district. Sparks' 140-foot shot tower, built in 1808 and still standing, is to the right of the dry dock. The dry dock could be pumped clear of water in an hour, and an 1800-ton merchantman could be docked in the same amount of time.

101
"Little Man," carved by Samuel Sailor of Philadelphia, ca. 1875. During the 18th and 19th centuries, particularly in England and America, carvings of naval and merchant officers served as shop signs for instrument sellers who had earned the respect of the seafaring community.

101

102

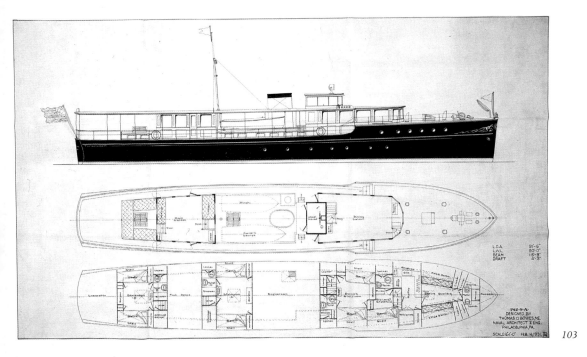

103

102
"Palace Steamer Republic,"
chromolithograph by E.P. and
L. Restein of Philadelphia, ca. 1890.
The splendid Republic was launched
by Harlan and Hollingsworth
Shipbuilding Co. of Wilmington in
1878. Her elegant service to Cape
May, New Jersey, did much to
popularize the resort town. The
Republic is shown here carrying
famous personalities, including
President Grover Cleveland, Lillian
Russell and Buffalo Bill.

103
"Lenore II," architectural drawing
by Thomas D. Bowes, 1931. Probably
the most famous design of
Philadelphia naval architect Bowes,
the Lenore II was built in 1931 for
Sewell Avery. Given to the Coast
Guard after the attack on Pearl
Harbor, the motor vessel went on to
serve as a private yacht to presidents
Truman, Eisenhower, and Kennedy.

104

Franklin, the Liberty Bell, or the Phillies, 76'ers, and the Flyers abound. Wharves, Kocks cranes, longshoremen, and container ships do not spring to mind.

Today, the "Ports of Philadelphia," which encompass the shipping facilities from Trenton, on the north, to Wilmington, Delaware, on the south, take their place with those of New York and Baltimore as the leading entrepôts of the North Atlantic East Coast. Such prominence is a residual legacy of three and a half centuries of unparalleled maritime activity on and alongside the bay and river.

It all began on August 28, 1609, when Henry Hudson, in the *Half Moon*, attempted to sail into Delaware Bay, found it to be full of treacherous shoals, and so ventured farther north in search of another body of water more to his liking. He was followed to the region

104
President Grover Cleveland presided over the christening of the North Atlantic steamship St. Louis, *built by William Cramp and Sons' Ship and Engine Building Co. Photograph by William H. Rease, 1894*

during the next fifty years by the Dutch, the Swedes, and the English. Eventually, because of the immense shipbuilding industry the Delaware River fostered in future years, the waterway came to be dubbed "the American Clyde," after the famous Scottish shipbuilding river of that name.

Philadelphia itself was founded by William Penn in 1682 and grew with such phenomenal vigor that it became, after London, the second largest English-speaking city in the world. Ships and shipping had been responsible for its fortunes. And at length, thanks to the city's nineteenth-century industrial complex—one miraculously capable of transforming the raw materials shipped thither into endless offerings of manufactured goods shipped right back out—the metropolis earned the sobriquet "Workshop of the World."

It was in Philadelphia in 1731 that Thomas Godfrey invented the precursor of the navigator's sextant—the octant—only to have the credit go to John Hadley, an Englishman who developed a comparable instrument simultaneously. And it was in Philadelphia where the designs were prepared not only for the first frigates of the Continental Navy during the American Revolution but also for those of the subsequent federal navy, including *Constitution* and *United States*, among others.

In 1787, John Fitch demonstrated at Philadelphia to George Washington and members of the Constitutional Convention his forty-five-foot steamboat, which was capable of achieving three knots; three years later, with an improved hull and engine, he inaugurated eight-mile-per-hour passenger service between the city's Arch Street Ferry and Trenton, New Jersey, although Robert Fulton's Hudson River steamboat of 1807 generally is given credit for commercializing nautical steam technology.

It is no wonder, then, that a need existed for a museum devoted to the collection, preservation, and interpretation of the maritime mementoes of the region's past. The Philadelphia Maritime Museum opened its doors to the public on May 19, 1961, as a result. Since that time, the museum has become the Delaware Valley's principal repository for its maritime heritage.

The brainchild of J. Welles Henderson, a Philadelphia attorney, the genesis of the new museum sprang from the success of an exhibition he had assembled at the Athenaeum of Philadelphia in 1955, as well as from the interest generated in 1957 by two major showings of his own Philadelphia maritime collections. Mounted first at the venerable Peabody Museum of Salem, Massachusetts, said to be the oldest museum in continuous operation in the United States, it was repeated a few months later at the Free Library of Philadelphia with equal success.

From his youth, Henderson had indulged his interest in local maritime history, and for years he had collected avidly in the field. It was then a time when he had relatively few competitors. Yet, at the same time, the ship portraits and the decorative arts of the

105
A silver ewer, made by M.W. Galt & Brother of Washington, D.C., was presented to Commodore E.A.F. Lavalette in 1858. Lavalette was awarded the Congressional Medal of Honor for his valor while serving under Captain Thomas Macdonough during the War of 1812. The ewer was given to him by the Washington Naval Yard.

106
This unusual epee includes two enameled scenes of victorious American naval actions of the War of 1812: the United States frigate Constitution *engaging the British* Guerriere, *and the* Constitution *battling the British* Java. *The epee was presented in 1815 to Commander James Biddle by his fellow Philadelphians, for meritorious service.*

107
Philadelphia merchant Benjamin Etting (1798–1875) was one of the many merchants who profited handsomely from American trade with China during the late 18th and early 19th century. Shown here is Etting's portrait—a miniature watercolor on ivory, by Hugh Bridport, ca. 1835, the journal kept by Etting on voyages to Canton, and a lacquered humidor made in Canton, ca. 1835.

108
The Irish-born merchant John Barry was one of the most distinguished and well-known captains of the first Continental Navy. The Philadelphia Maritime Museum has in its collections John Barry's gold and agate fob seal, attributed to James Musgrove, ca. 1775; a manuscript from Barry to John Brown of Philadelphia, with the Barry seal; and a porcelain with John Barry's cipher, made in Canton.

105

106

107

108

109

110

111

109

Among the more beautiful ship models in the collection of the Philadelphia Maritime Museum is that of the 120-gun British ship-of-the-line Caledonia. The model, over 42 inches long, is built entirely of bone and rests on an inlaid wooden base encircled with a bone railing. Some bone models were built by American, British, and French prisoners-of-war during the American Revolution and the Napoleonic Wars, but the delicacy and detail of this one suggest the hand of a master, perhaps an early-19th-century French craftsman from Dieppe. The HMS Caledonia was, at the time of its launching in 1808, the largest warship built, setting the standard for the next generation of British first-raters.

110

Dating from the decade after World War I, this enameled tin boat was one of many manufactured in Germany by Märklin and Co. The model is supposed to represent the USS Baltimore, but it is, in fact, a "generic" cruiser type on which any name might be painted.

111

The original Shamokin, a sturdy workhorse and winner of the 1952 and 1953 New York Harbor Tugboat Championships, was designed in 1950 by leading naval architect Thomas D. Bowes of Philadelphia. This model was built by George Snyder in 1984.

112

112
Smallest of the four Hiker classes of Delaware River racing sailboats, the tuck up flourished during the last half of the 19th century, when small boat regattas were the popular spectator sport. The boat derives its name from the unique manner in which its plank keel "tucks up" into the transom. This reproduction was built in 1986 at the Philadelphia Maritime Museum's Workshop on the Water by boatbuilders John Brady, John Tohanczyn, and a crew of volunteers.

Philadelphia mariner were few and far between. To understand why that should have been so, it is necessary to recall that, unlike other maritime centers of the early republic, such as those in the New England states, Philadelphia's pervasive Quaker disapproval of ostentatious display precluded their creation in comparable numbers.

Despite these difficulties, Henderson managed to accumulate an extraordinary personal collection of books, paintings, and artifacts. Significant pieces from his collection which served to initiate the Philadelphia Maritime Museum's exhibition material were added to the institutional collections periodically.

The original displays were housed in a rented room in the Athenaeum of Philadelphia, on Washington Square, just around the corner from Independence Hall and Philadelphia's most historic area. Although the site was excellent for the purposes of attracting tourists, by 1964 more commodious quarters seemed to be in order. A year later, a newly incorporated nonprofit Philadelphia Maritime Museum had opened its doors at 427 Chestnut Street in two rented nineteenth-century bank buildings opposite the Second Bank of the United States building in Independence Park. And finally, at the end of 1970, the decision was made by the museum's governing Board of Port Wardens to purchase a building of its own. Located one block closer to the Delaware River than before but still opposite Independence Park and the core of tourism, 321 Chestnut Street has continued to serve as the museum's headquarters since its initial galleries were opened to the public, but as the museum continues to expand, even these facilities may be outgrown in time.

113
Among the earliest surviving examples of American shipcarving is the ''fancy work''—the figurehead, trailboards, the stern and quarter gallery carving—on Joshua Humphreys's 1777 dockyard model for a proposed 74-gun ship-of-the-line for the Continental Navy. Although he was a peace-loving Quaker, Humphreys designed warships at Philadelphia during the American Revolution and later became first Chief Naval Constructor of the United States. He was intimately concerned with the design and building of many of the nation's first frigates.

114
Although the name of the vessel for which Philadelphia's William Rush (1756–1833) carved this elegant figurehead is unknown, the ca. 1805 sculpture is called ''Peace.'' Rush was, during his lifetime, America's most skilled carver. A number of his non-marine pieces can be seen in public collections throughout Philadelphia.

114

In an informal expression of its character, Henderson once wrote of the institution: "The Museum is international in scope, national in theme, and regional in emphasis." Its collections, a number of them truly unique in the world of maritime museums, reflect that spirit.

From the very beginning of its settlement, the Delaware Valley became justly famed for the vessels it built, now evoking for the student of such matters such names as Humphreys, Grice, Wharton, Harlan & Hollingsworth, Pusey & Jones, Roach, Sun Ship, New York Ship, Dialogue, Mathis, Cramp, and many, many others. In the late eighteenth century it was claimed by some that the best ship in the world would have a Boston underbody and Philadelphia topsides, a plain suggestion that if Boston built ships for speed, Philadelphia built them for beauty.

It is a long road of human endeavor from Joshua Humphreys's elegant half-hull model of 1777 (for a proposed but never built 74-gun ship for the Continental Navy) to the plating model for the nuclear-powered merchant ship *Savannah*, built by New York Shipbuilding Corporation, Camden, New Jersey, in the late 1950s. Yet both may be found in the museum's collections, together with photographs, prints, plans, additional artifacts, and manuscripts pertaining to the region's all-but-vanished shipyards and such well-known designer-builders as Humphreys himself, John Lenthall, John Roach, and naval architect Thomas David Bowes.

No one can say exactly how many vessels have been launched into the Delaware River over the years, but it has been estimated that during the two centuries between the battles of Lexington and Concord in 1775 and the United States' Bicentennial year of 1976, Delaware Valley shipyards built 948 naval vessels of all classes, including a few for foreign governments. The period of World War II, alone, accounts for 534. One cannot forget, either, the monumental World War I facility created from scratch on Hog Island in less than ten months, where fifty shipways, twenty outfitting basins, 300 freight cars of materials daily, and 35,000 workers cranked out 122 Hog Island freighters within only three years.

The museum does not engage in ship construction, but it does maintain a boat-building workshop at Penn's Landing, on the riverfront, for the study and building of small craft, especially tuck ups, rail-bird skiffs, garveys, duckers, and other boat types indigenous to the region. This facility, aptly named "Workshop on the Water," is the museum's largest artifact, a 110-foot house-covered steel lighter barge built in 1935 for work on the Delaware River. Acquired during the autumn of 1980, the barge *Maple* was transformed during the next several years into the museum's workshop and now regularly attracts a burgeoning following of small craft builders and "hands-on" boat enthusiasts. Workshop staff assemble seasonal exhibitions to revive interest in the use and construction of local traditional small boats and boating activities.

115
"First Settlement of the Swedes in Christiana River," by George Robert Bonfield of Philadelphia, 1861. Heading a government-backed but private Swedish exploring company, Peter Minuit, with two vessels under his command, stepped ashore alongside the Christiana and Delaware rivers in 1638. The landing site became Wilmington, Delaware. One of Minuit's two ships, the Kalmar Nyckel, *dominates this landing scene.*

115

116
"Philadelphia from Camden, 1850,"
chromolithograph by W. Hill and
Smith, 1850. The best view of
Philadelphia has always been from its
neighbor, Camden, New Jersey, across
the Delaware River. The islands in
mid-stream, Windmill (left) *and*
Smith's (right), *were removed during*
the 1890s to enhance navigation and
permit expansion of Philadelphia's
pierhead line. Ferries serviced
Pennsylvania and New Jersey for a
number of years even after the
Benjamin Franklin Bridge opened in
1926.

The only other floating artifact in the institution's history has been the three-masted Portuguese barkentine *Gazela Primeiro*, thought to have been built in 1883. Acquired for the museum in 1970 by a major benefactor, the late William Wikoff Smith, this majestic square-rigger was owned by the Philadelphia Maritime Museum for a decade until soaring costs, prohibitive insurance premiums, and Coast Guard prohibitions against her use in sail training made it impossible for an eleemosynary institution to retain her. She is currently owned and operated by the city of Philadelphia as the *Gazela of Philadelphia*, a roving goodwill ambassadress.

In 1968, at its former location, the museum opened what was then considered to be the first gallery in the world to trace comprehensively the history of man's progressive

ability to work and live underwater. From ancient free-diving techniques and salvage operations by diving bell to more modern developments in hard hat and self-contained underwater breathing apparatus (SCUBA) technology, exploratory submersibles, and habitats on the sea floor, the exhibition probed human accomplishments in taming inner space. Even though no longer shown publicly on a permanent basis, the artifacts remain part of the museum's study collections.

In a related area, even if not fully recognized as such until the summers of 1985 and 1986, when Dr. Robert Ballard of the Woods Hole Oceanographic Institute discovered the seventy-three-year-old remains of the White Star liner R.M.S. *Titanic*, are the pre-sinking artifacts collected over the years by the 3,000-member Titanic Historical Society. These

117
''View of Philadelphia,'' by Thomas Birch, 1841. Birch undertook several views of Philadelphia's Delaware River waterfront, of which this is one. At the far left are the ship houses of the old Philadelphia Navy Yard and Sparks' shot tower. The abundance of shipping—sail and steam—suggests the constant activity at the port.

CUTTER YACHT "SCUD".
OF PHILADELPHIA.

were installed at the museum on permanent deposit in April 1982 for the Society's Philadelphia convention, which marked the seventieth anniversary of the disaster.

Among the many items on continuing exhibit are a salvaged deck chair; Mrs. John Jacob Astor's life jacket; the discharge book of Frederick Fleet, the lookout who first sighted the iceberg; a Marconigram from S.S. *Amerika* warning the *Titanic* of ice in her path; personal memorabilia of passengers and crew; actual stationery from the *Titanic*; and a small square of green carpeting from the First Class accommodations.

From earliest colonial times until the passing of the wooden sailing ship in the twentieth century, a majority of vessels were adorned with ornamental carvings: figureheads and billetheads, cathead faces, trailboards, gangway boards, stern and quarter-gallery embellishments, and the like. Any shipbuilding community of consequence boasted a cadre of skilled ship carvers, and Philadelphia was no exception. Exclusive of the occasional dabbler in the field, or laborers and apprentices who later plied the trade

118
"Cutter Yacht Scud *of Philadelphia," chromolithograph by J.E. Buttersworth and C. Parsons for N. Currier, 1855. From small boat clubs up and down the Delaware River to the prestigious Corinthian Yacht Club at Essington, area residents have always used their waterways for pleasure. Area shipyards produced many of the turn-of-the-century grand yachts for customers throughout the country. Here, the cutter yacht* Scud, *built by Albertson's yard, Philadelphia, races the cutter* Fawn.

119

elsewhere, there were at least twenty-six master woodcarvers at work in Philadelphia and its immediate vicinity between the end of the first decade of the eighteenth century and the mid nineteenth.

One of the lesser-known Philadelphia practitioners was Samuel Sailor, active from about 1858 to 1875, who also happened to be the last of particular note in the city. The only known surviving example of his work is a carved figure of a ship's officer taking a meridional sight with his sextant. From the mid-1870s until the early 1970s, this carving served as a shop sign for Riggs & Brother, nautical instrument sellers of Philadelphia. It has now become something of a mascot for the Philadelphia Maritime Museum.

Sailor's chunky, severe style suggests a mathematical, uninspired, almost childlike rendition of nature, more akin to the rigidity of much eighteenth-century carving than to late nineteenth-century work. Few carvers achieved enduring fame for their ability to breathe the appearance of life into wood. Among these, however, perhaps the ultimate

119
In this original rendering for the frontispiece to Our Navy, Its Growth and Achievement, *written by Jerrold Kelly, marine artist Frederick S. Cozzens depicts the Columbian Naval Review of 1893, in which Philadelphia-built vessels* Atlanta, Philadelphia, *and* Newark *played a prominent role.*

craftsman in the genre—and one whose clients were by no means limited to shipowners—was Philadelphia's William Rush (1756–1833). Rush can be credited with the carving of at least forty-two figureheads, but only three of these can now be located, either by certain knowledge or attribution. The museum owns one of the three, the only full-length figure, known as ''Peace'' and attributed to Rush by virtue of the breezy, free-flowing treatment of volume that sets him apart from his colleagues.

Among the museum's collections are plans, photographs, and business records of Cramp shipyard, Sun Shipbuilding, and New York Ship. Additionally, the museum library houses the private library of John Lenthall, one of the first naval constructors, and papers of John Barry and John Green. Personal items once belonging to famous naval heroes Stephen Decatur, James Biddle, and E. A. F. Lavalette are also found among the museum's holdings.

The *Empress of China*, the first American vessel to initiate trade with the Chinese, was financed from Philadelphia. The first American vessel to trade with India hailed from Philadelphia. The first steam-powered icebreaker was built alongside the Delaware River and was powered by an engine constructed by Philadelphia's Matthias W. Baldwin, later famed for the manufacture of railroad locomotives. In 1861, two years after Colonel Edwin Drake brought in the first commercially viable oil well in the country, the first cargo of petroleum shipped out of the United States left the Delaware River bound for London.

Whether ''first'' or not, Philadelphia's role in the history of North American shipping should not be underestimated. The deplorable fact is that too many visitors to the city are unaware of the water flowing by it: water ever in motion, water ever busy, water half a mile wide. As for many Philadelphians themselves, pride in their city's extraordinary maritime tradition requires some rekindling. Thus it is that the Philadelphia Maritime Museum exists to educate the resident and the tourist alike to the city's grand history of maritime enterprise.

120
''Shad Fishing at Gloucester, New Jersey, on the Delaware River—Seine Haul,'' photograph by Thomas C. Eakins, ca. 1881. Eakins (1844–1916), one of Philadelphia's most beloved artists, may be best known for his works that depict sculling on the Schuylkill River, but he also observed the spring shad fishing season along the Delaware River. He executed a number of paintings and drawings to illustrate the commercial pursuit of these succulent fish.

THE CALVERT MARINE MUSEUM

The Calvert Marine Museum

SOLOMONS · MARYLAND

The Calvert Marine Museum is situated beside a picturesque estuary at the confluence of the Patuxent River and Chesapeake Bay. It is most appropriate that a marine museum be located at this spot, in a region that is steeped in maritime history and surrounded by rich marine resources. The Patuxent is the longest intrastate river in Maryland, reaching a length of over one hundred miles and draining approximately 10 percent of the state's land surface. The river flows through the heart of excellent tobacco-growing soils, and this, coupled with the river's deep, natural channel and numerous tributaries, contributed to its early development as a maritime trading center in the mid-seventeenth century.

The Patuxent's history involves maritime military activity as well. Maryland's largest naval engagement, the Battle of St. Leonard Creek, took place during the War of 1812, when the British used the river for access to Washington, D.C., the only time our nation's capital ever fell into enemy hands. Because the mouth of the river is one of the deepest natural harbors on the east coast of the United States, it was selected in 1905 to test the world's largest dry dock at that time, the *Dewey*. The *Dewey* dry dock successfully lifted the battleships USS *Maryland*, USS *Iowa*, and the armored cruiser USS *Colorado*, the largest ships of their day. And from 1927 to 1940, the river also served as home to four interned German ocean liners, including the *George Washington*, upon which President Wilson had traveled to Versailles, France, in 1919 to sign the treaty ending World War I.

During World War II, the U.S. Navy took advantage of the Patuxent's deep water and sheltered anchorages to establish the nation's first amphibious training base at Solomons. Curiously, marines who trained here made the successful landings later on the Solomon Islands in the Pacific. The Patuxent near Solomons was also the site of the Naval Weapons Mines Test Center. Mines and torpedoes used during World War II, the Korean War, and in Vietnam were tested in the 100-foot depths near the river's mouth. Also

121
Preceding pages: *Drum Point Lighthouse and grounds of the Calvert Marine Museum from Back Creek*

122
Workboats and a heron in a Patuxent River sunset, 1982

124

123

during World War II, just across the river, the Patuxent Naval Air Station was established. Many test pilots were trained at that facility, including astronaut John Glenn.

Commerce on the river has taken many forms, but perhaps the liveliest era of commercial activity took place during the Chesapeake oystering boom of the late nineteenth and early twentieth centuries. Oyster packers and entrepreneurs flocked to the lower Patuxent, where they established commercial enterprises for buying, packing, and shipping the local seafood bounty. Shipbuilders came as well and, before long, Solomons became an important center for wooden boatbuilding. Indeed, shipyards in Solomons produced more bugeyes, the famed two-masted vessels designed for dredging oysters in the shallow waters of the Chesapeake, than any other community on the Bay. At the turn of the century, Thomas Moore of Solomons reputedly owned the largest private fleet on the Bay, numbering nearly one hundred fishing and oystering vessels.

123
Drum Point Lighthouse keeper William Yeatman with his children, September 9, 1918. The wooden bridge at left connects the lighthouse to the shore.

124
(Left) Chesapeake Bay skipjack; (right) bugeye; (background) schooner

125

126

127

Solomons held its distinction as a center for boatbuilding well beyond the oyster bonanza. During the 1930s, the M. M. Davis & Son Shipyard brought international fame to the region by building numerous fine wooden yachts and racing vessels. Perhaps best known was the yacht *Manitou*, built by M. M. Davis & Son in 1937 and later sailed by President John F. Kennedy.

As are many coastal areas of the United States, the Patuxent basin is experiencing profound economic, environmental, and cultural changes. Wooden boatbuilding is practically a thing of the past, and the commercial fisheries are imperiled by a combination of polluted waters and decades of intensive harvesting. The Patuxent is no longer a route for commerce or trade, but is instead a recreational mecca for pleasure boaters, sport fishermen, and tourists. However, the rich maritime heritage of the region is being documented, preserved, and interpreted through the efforts of the Calvert Marine Museum.

125
The oyster-packing room at J. C. Lore & Sons in Solomons, ca. 1935. The Calvert Marine Museum now owns the former oyster house and has restored its packing room.

126
The Thomas Moore shipyard in Solomons, 1901.

127
M. M. Davis & Son shipyard in Solomons during World War I. A 7000-ton barge is under construction at right.

In 1970, the Calvert County Historical Society established the Calvert Marine Museum. Today the museum occupies a nine-acre site with six buildings and an annex museum of another acre with two buildings. The main exhibit building is appropriately housed in the former Solomons High School, thus giving new life to the educational purpose of the building. Interestingly, between 1925 and 1935 many children reached the school via a converted oyster boat, the *James Aubrey*. The school boat's original mast serves as the museum's flagpole.

Standing over the old school dock is the Drum Point Lighthouse, which dominates the waterfront. Constructed in 1883 at Drum Point, which marks the entrance to the Patuxent River on the north, this screwpile, cottage-type light is one of the only three

128
The skipjack Dee of St. Mary's *dredges for oysters in Chesapeake Bay near Calvert Cliffs, 1983. The* Dee *is one of approximately twenty-five sailing skipjacks still in use as oyster dredgers in Maryland.*

remaining from forty-five which served the Chesapeake Bay at the turn of the century. Decommissioned in 1962, the lighthouse was moved two nautical miles to the museum by barge and tug in 1975. The structure has been authentically restored to its appearance as it was in 1900, thanks in part to the efforts of Anna Weems Ewalt, a local resident who was born in the lighthouse. Original furnishings include the china used by Ewalt's grandfather while he was the light keeper, the original fog bell and lens, and the chair used by the last civilian light keeper at Drum Point, John Hansen. The Drum Point Lighthouse is listed on the National Register of Historic Places.

Within the shadow of the lighthouse lies the berth for the museum's excursion vessel, the *Wm. B. Tennison*. The hull of this sixty-one-foot vessel is constructed of nine

129
Recreational fishing in the Patuxent River near the Thomas Johnson bridge, 1982

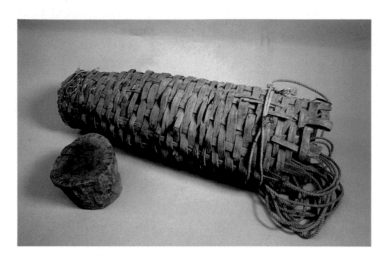

130   131

logs. The *Tennison* was built as a sailing bugeye in 1899 and in 1911 was converted to an oyster buyboat. She bought oysters from working vessels and hauled them to shucking houses in winter. In summer she hauled fruit, vegetables, and other freight between the tidewater towns and cities of the Chesapeake. From 1941 to 1978, the *Tennison* dredged and bought oysters for the J. C. Lore & Sons oyster house, located in Solomons. Since 1979, when she was acquired by the museum, the *Tennison* has provided cruises around Solomons harbor and the Patuxent River for museum visitors. The *Wm. B. Tennison* is the oldest U.S. Coast Guard–licensed passenger vessel in the Chesapeake Bay and third oldest in the United States. The *Tennison* is also listed on the National Register of Historic Places.

Between the lighthouse and the main exhibit building lies the boat basin, a 200-by-200-foot protected area where historic small craft are displayed, including the skipjack *Marie Theresa*, built in 1906. In this picturesque inlet, members of the museum-sponsored Solomons Island Model Boat Club race scale-model, remote-controlled skipjacks. The boatbuilding skills preservation center, where Patuxent Small Craft Guild members build and demonstrate traditional craft of the region, such as log punts and double-ended crab skiffs, stands adjacent to the basin. A small craft shed sits near the basin and houses historic vessels such as the *Bar Dog*, a rare two-log canoe; *John A. Ryder*, a deadrise power workboat outfitted with the first clam dredge used in the Chesapeake; and the *Let's See*, a Potomac River dory which represents one of the last of her type on the Bay.

Nearby is a woodworking shop where visitors can see and talk to the museum's resident master woodcarver, "Pepper" Langley, who carves trailboards, stern decorations, and an occasional figurehead. In the same building the museum's resident modelmaker, Jimmy Langley, can be seen building models of local watercraft. "Pepper" and Jimmy Langley, who are father and son, respectively, pass along their considerable skills to

130
This handmade eelpot, woven of oak splints, is one of several types of eelpots in the fisheries collection at Calvert Marine Museum. Chesapeake Bay watermen caught eels in wooden traps like this until the 1920s, when they began using wire eelpots.

131
A typical wooden duck decoy from the collections of Calvert Marine Museum

132

133

A Chesapeake Bay workboat under construction in southern Maryland, 1983

This 16-foot, flat-bottom crabbing skiff was used by Captain Harry Benning of Galesville, Maryland, for crabbing and gill-net fishing. She was originally powered by sail, but around 1920 Benning replaced her sail rig with a gasoline engine. The museum's small craft shed, which contains twenty vessels, is visible behind the skiff.

members of the Southern Maryland Shipcarvers' Guild, another museum-sponsored club.

The permanent exhibits of the museum seek to describe the work techniques of watermen through such displays as a partially reconstructed oyster-shucking shed from the Sollers and Dowell Company and a typical wharf where workboats would have off-loaded their catch. A maritime history room is dominated by the twenty-eight-foot-long Poquoson log canoe *Carla Sue*, while the other side of the room is occupied by a reconstructed shipbuilder's lean-to from the M. M. Davis Shipyard. This lean-to features a wide range of shipbuilding tools, including woodworking planes, caulking irons, pitch pots, adzes, and sailmaking gear. Decorative wood carvings, such as trailboards and figureheads, boat models, photographs, and paintings interpret the region's maritime history, with a special emphasis on local shipbuilding and steamboating on the Patuxent River.

The Calvert Marine Museum's changing exhibits include watercolor and oil paintings by the late Chesapeake Bay artist, Louis J. Feuchter (1885–1957), watercolors depicting the history of sail by Cmdr. E. C. Tufnell (1888–1979), mixed-media paintings of steamboats by Joseph S. Bohannon (1894–1973), and photographic prints depicting southern Maryland scenes by Baltimore *Sunday Sun* photographer A. Aubrey Bodine (1906–1970).

Other exhibits include sports fishing, marine engines, decoys, and a unique collection of diving gear, including a rare U.S. Navy World War I Northill rebreather, several World War II rebreathers, and SCUBA and hard hat examples.

"War on the Patuxent: 1814," an exhibit interpreting the heroic attempt of America's Chesapeake Flotilla to defend the Chesapeake against Royal Navy forces during the War of 1812, is an example of the museum's efforts to literally plumb the depths of the area's maritime history. Many of these artifacts were recovered through underwater archaeology from one of the Flotilla vessels which fought in a most strategic naval engagement—protecting the United States capital.

A submerged cultural resource survey of the Patuxent River was begun in 1978 by the Calvert Marine Museum and Nautical Archaeological Associates, Inc. This three-year project resulted in the first holistic approach to an underwater archaeological survey in Maryland and the first predictive model for submerged cultural resources in a riverine system in the United States. The first underwater archaeological permit ever issued by the State of Maryland resulted in the discovery of the Chesapeake Flotilla artifacts. In addition, over one hundred shipwrecks were documented in the Patuxent River, as well as numerous inundated prehistoric and historic sites such as Indian encampments and wharves. The Lyon's Creek Site may represent one of the earliest small-craft wreck sites in the United States, dating from 1680 to 1730. Hundreds of artifacts recovered during the

134
Exterior of the former J.C. Lore & Sons oyster house, now part of the Calvert Marine Museum. The building is on the National Register of Historic Places and houses exhibits on the Patuxent River seafood industries.

course of this survey are now conserved and preserved in the collections of the Calvert Marine Museum, a handful of which are on display to the visitor.

One-half mile down the road on Solomons Island proper is the J. C. Lore & Sons oyster house, another museum facility. The present building dates from 1934, replacing an earlier structure destroyed by a severe storm in 1933. J. C. Lore & Sons, Inc., was the longest continuously operating seafood-packing house on the Patuxent River. When it closed in 1978, due in part to the diminishing harvests of high-quality local oysters, the museum felt compelled to acquire and preserve the structure that had been so important to the Patuxent fisheries. The building is now listed on the National Register of Historic Places, and houses two major exhibits on the commercial seafood industries and on the present traditions of wooden workboat building in the region. Featured are the distinctive designs of four local boatbuilders as well as a wide range of artifacts from the museum's vast fisheries collection, including tools and gear used by Chesapeake Bay watermen for harvesting oysters, crabs, soft-shell clams, eels, and fish, and processing equipment used by local businesses for packing seafood products. In these exhibits, the vigorous work and way of life characteristic of the Patuxent's water-oriented communities is shown, supplemented by historic and contemporary photographs and with materials collected in 1981–82 for the Patuxent River Folklife and Oral History Project, during which museum researchers conducted tape-recorded interviews with local watermen, workboat builders, packinghouse workers, and lifelong residents of river communities.

Behind the oyster house is a re-creation of the Benning Lime Company oyster-shell crushing mill that was once located in Galesville, Maryland. The actual mill machinery was dismantled and reassembled in a new building. Oyster shells, an oyster byproduct, were used as road metal, fertilizer, and chicken feed. In fact, the mill and oyster house

135
Chesapeake Bay watermen oystering with hydraulic patent tongs near Solomons, 1982

136
The Wm. B. Tennison, *built in 1899 for dredging oysters in Chesapeake Bay, is now a tour boat for visitors to the Calvert Marine Museum.*

137
Pound-net fishermen emptying their net in the Patuxent River, 1982

138
The waters behind the restored J.C. Lore & Sons oyster house occasionally harbor Chesapeake Bay skipjacks during the winter oystering season.

139
The Chesapeake Bay crabbing scrape, Geda, *in the calm waters of St. Leonard Creek, Maryland. The* Geda *is now in the small craft collection at Calvert Marine Museum. Crabbing scrapes were the forerunners of Chesapeake Bay skipjacks.*

135   136

137

138   *139*

stand on shells shucked and discarded over the years, creating new land which eventually helped to join Solomons Island to the mainland.

At beautiful Flag Ponds Nature Park, located nine miles north of the main museum complex on the Chesapeake Bay, the museum interprets one of the major pound-net fishing camps, once numerous along the Bay. A fisherman's shanty, the "Buoy Hotel No. 2" dating from the 1920s, contains an exhibit about this fishery that operated at the site from 1915 to 1958. From there, a "Fisherman's Trail" leads to such points of interest as net tarring stations and former docks.

As the museum's name implies, the Calvert Marine Museum is not solely a maritime museum but one that interprets both the environmental and cultural marine history of the region and seeks to illuminate the prehistoric and present environment of the area, such as the world-famous Calvert Cliffs, one of the richest deposits of marine Miocene fossils in the world. From the cliffs come ten- to seventeen-million-year-old fossils of porpoises, whales, seals, sharks, crabs, and hundreds of different mollusks. Also on view is a half-scale model of a *Pelagornis*, an extinct false-toothed, pelicanlike bird with a wingspan of eighteen to twenty-two feet, the largest marine bird known. An exhibit focusing on the estuarine life of the Patuxent River includes aquariums with living displays, mounted fish, birds, semi-aquatic mammals, and a "touch table."

This is an exciting time in the history of the Calvert Marine Museum. It is going through an era of major growth, including expansion of the library, collections storage, conservation, and exhibition facilities. The museum's capacity to record and interpret the unique history of the Patuxent River region's maritime heritage is being dramatically increased. Indeed, though they never would have guessed it, part of the story of the expanding Calvert Marine Museum is the work, the lives, and the heritage of the watermen, oyster shuckers, and steamboat captains who toiled along the waters of the Patuxent from earliest times.

140
Between 1927 and 1940 four German luxury liners captured during World War I were anchored near the mouth of the Patuxent River. Known as the Ghost Fleet, the four ships provided a dramatic contrast to the rural setting. Here dairy cows from a nearby farm cool off in the river with the Ghost Fleet looming in the distance.

THE MARINERS' MUSEUM

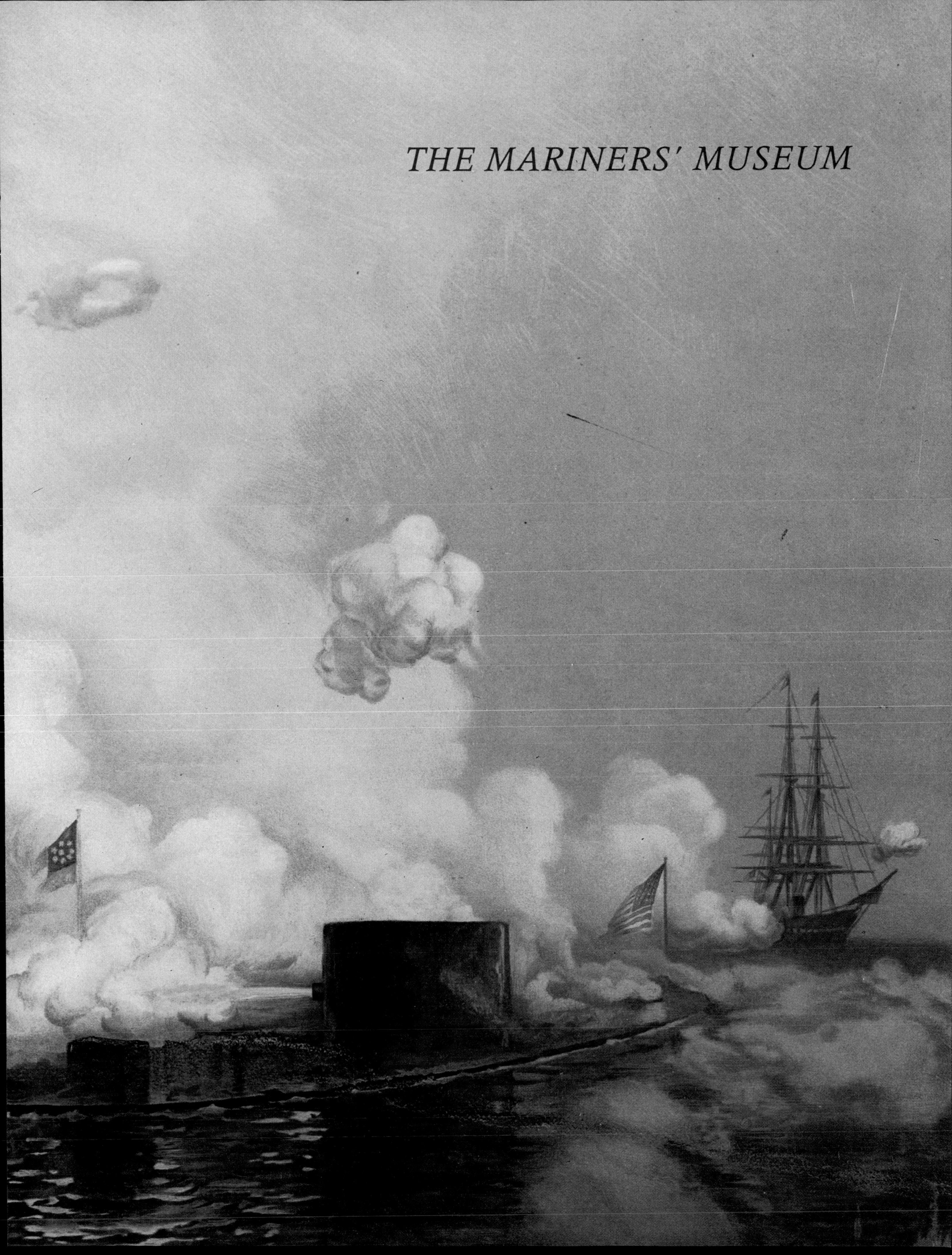

8 *Man and Sea:*
International Maritime History
at The Mariners' Museum
Richard C. Malley, Associate Curator

The Mariners' Museum

NEWPORT NEWS · VIRGINIA

"An inland sea" it has been called by some, this vast body of water known as Chesapeake Bay. An arm of the sea formed by the drowned path of the Susquehanna River, this remarkable bay extends its influence through a vast hinterland by means of many rivers that, spokelike, project out in all directions.

A splendid means of communication; a rich storehouse of food; a strategic prize contested by friend and foe; a source of livelihood and recreation; a natural barometer of the quality of life: Chesapeake Bay is this and more, a true microcosm of the sea. At the Bay's southern end, where open Atlantic meets estuarial Chesapeake, is one of the finest natural anchorages in the world, Hampton Roads. Its economic and strategic value over the centuries has made it a crossroads for world maritime commerce and a bastion of naval power.

It was along the shore of this roadstead, in Newport News, Virginia, in 1930 that scholar and philanthropist Archer M. Huntington decided to establish a maritime museum dedicated to preserving the culture of the sea in all its aspects. His father, railroad magnate Collis P. Huntington, had helped to create Newport News by extending his C & O Railroad to its undeveloped shores in the 1880s. The elder Huntington's subsequent founding of a shipyard placed the small port town on the map for keeps. In time, watermen working the area's rich oyster and crab grounds found themselves sharing their local waters with merchant ships from around the world and all manner of newly launched commercial and naval vessels.

Archer Huntington's creation, the Mariners' Museum, reflects the dual identity of the Hampton Roads area, at once a major international port in touch with the outside world and an area with its own distinct maritime tradition. Over three thousand years of nautical experience on stream, bay, and ocean is represented in the museum's fourteen

141
Preceding pages: *The nightmarish 1862 engagement between the ironclads* Monitor *and* Merrimac *is brought vividly to life in this 1886 chromolithograph. Based on a painting by Julian O. Davidson (1853–94), it captures the intensity of the battle that forever altered the face of naval warfare.*

142
Looking for all the world like the figure of Columbia, this 8-foot-tall figurehead once graced the bow of the British full-rigged iron ship Benmore, *built in 1870. The strikingly patriotic paint scheme was applied after the vessel was purchased by an American firm in 1920.*

galleries. More than a half century of careful collecting has produced a splendid chronicle, in word, artifact, and image, of the sea's influence on man.

Perhaps no finer representations can be found of the types of ships that have been built or have called at Hampton Roads than the superb ship models filling the museum's Great Hall of Steam. Representing but a small part of the model collection, some of these professionally built models have graced the boardrooms of major shipping lines, while others were constructed by the museum's own model shop in the 1930s. In walking through the hall one can trace the development of steam navigation from Fulton's *Clermont* of 1807 to a container ship of the 1970s. Along the way, legendary passenger liners like *Britannic*, *America*, *Mauretania*, and *Queen Elizabeth* are recalled in oversize models. Franklin D. Roosevelt, himself an avid maritime student and collector, recognized

143
The equivalent of nearly four years of work went into the construction of this model of a 17th-century Venetian galleass. One of August F. Crabtree's most impressive works, the model features 359 figures carved in low relief on panels at the bow and stern.

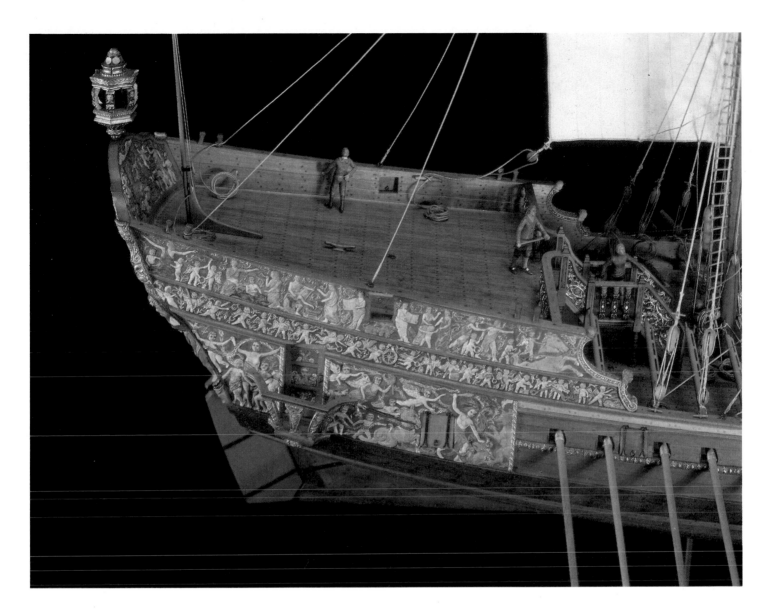

the significance of this exhibit when he donated an impressive model of the 1908 liner *Rotterdam*. Specialized exhibits on the SS *United States* and the ill-fated *Titanic* complement the cased models.

Man's many uses of the ship model are examined through examples as varied as a shipbuilder's half model, a nineteenth-century church memorial "votive" model, cast lead World War II warship recognition training models, and a large sailing model of a yacht. Models are seen in all their wide variety, from a miniature sealskin kayak fashioned by a Greenland Eskimo to a spectacular gold and silver music box model of the Long Island Sound steamboat *Commonwealth* crafted in the 1860s as a retirement gift for her master.

Of special significance is the August F. Crabtree collection of ship models. Sixteen

144
A close look at August F. Crabtree's Venetian galleass model reveals some of the 359 carved figures on the hull. Little wonder that the model required years to complete.

models illustrating the evolution of vessel design, from the makeshift log raft to the development of the ocean steamer, comprise this group. Twenty-eight years of painstaking research, material selection, and specialized tool development by Mr. Crabtree has resulted in a breathtaking collection of intricately carved and constructed miniatures. Not one to rest idly on his laurels, octogenarian Crabtree presents Sunday lectures at the museum describing his life's work.

Symbolism often overlaps function in nautical artifacts, and ships' figureheads provide a good example of this fact. The traditional painted or carved bow design, common in many seafaring cultures, found some of its most impressive expressions at the hands of European and, later, American shipcarvers. In American pine or European oak, freestanding or attached, upright or forward-raked, full- or half-length, such carvings helped to provide the "soul" of a vessel. By representing the human, mythological, or allegorical namesake of a ship, the figurehead often helped transform a floating mass of timbers and fastenings into a distinct entity.

A particularly noteworthy example is an immense gold-leafed American eagle, circa 1880, from the steam frigate USS *Lancaster*. The only identified, surviving figurehead by noted carver John H. Bellamy, this thirty-two-hundred-pound carving, with its eighteen-foot wingspan, now greets visitors entering the museum. Its massive grace clearly conveys the sense of power and dignity intended by its creator.

The museum's collection of such carvings, believed to be the single largest in the country, provides an eye-opening introduction to this specialized art form. But figureheads and their more modest scrollwork successors, billetheads, serve another function. Due to the shipboard placement of such carvings, their sizes and shapes tend to reflect basic differences or evolutions in vessel design. For example, a small, upright, bust-length figurehead like that of Commodore Morris, from the bluff-bowed whaleship of the same name, contrasts with the forward-raked, full-length, lifesize carving from the sleek medium clipper ship *Galatea*. To the discerning eye, then, such carvings can represent a splendid mixture of art and science.

Among the more well-known nautical folk art forms exhibited at the museum is scrimshaw, by which sailors, and especially whalemen, created decorative and utilitarian articles from the byproducts of the whale and walrus. Sperm whale teeth engraved with nautical, geometric, or sentimental images are perhaps the most familiar specimens of this art. However, pie crimpers and other kitchen utensils, yarn-winding swifts, corset busks, and canes are all examples of functional gifts wrought from the ivory, bone, and baleen of sea mammals. Ironically, what was primarily a time-killing diversion for bored seamen has become a subject of considerable interest to scholars and casual visitors alike.

The decorative arts have long reflected man's abiding interest in the sea. In the nineteenth century the advent of mass production techniques made such items available

145
The documenting of America's maritime heritage sometimes involves unusual means. This Liverpool creamware jug, part of a superb decorative arts collection, depicts the Virginia-built ship Orozimbo *of 1805. One of only two known examples, the* Orozimbo *jug testifies to the early growth of shipbuilding on Chesapeake Bay.*

OROZIMBO, OF BALTIMORE.

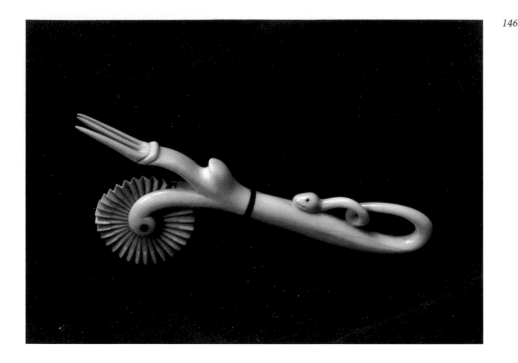

to a wider, more diverse, audience. In Britain especially, with its particularly strong maritime tradition, all manner of earthenware and porcelain objects bearing sea imagery were produced for both domestic and foreign markets. The early effects of the industrial revolution, combined with a strong colonial and foreign trade system, enabled Britain to produce and market ceramics like Staffordshire ware. America was a major purchaser of such consumer goods, as evidenced by the amount yet found in many homes and museums in this country. A wide sampling of these goods, some commemorative, some sentimental, and some humorous, fills an entire gallery, allowing visitors a sea experience of a different kind.

Artists have depicted the sea and ships from at least the time of the ancient Egyptians. By the late Middle Ages marine painting as a distinct form began to develop in Europe, largely reflecting the classical tastes of the aristocracy. But the rise of a middle class in the eighteenth century ushered in a new era—and type—of marine art. Successful merchants, shipowners, or naval officers, wishing to memorialize the sources of their wealth or fame, helped spawn a corps of ship portraitists in many European ports. In time such painters appeared in America, too; men such as Robert Salmon, James Buttersworth, James Bard, and Antonio Jacobsen. To such artists is owed a debt of gratitude for visually documenting hundreds of vessels that might otherwise have remained simply names in a register.

146
Scrimshaw items can combine both decorative and utilitarian elements. This 7-inch-long serpentine-carved whale ivory jagging wheel includes a dark band of tortoise shell. As with most examples of this nautical folk art, the "scrimshander" remains anonymous.

147
The sperm whale tooth provided the "canvas" for many a whaleman, and one of the most popular subjects for these shipboard artists was women. Whether engraved freehand or, as on this 8-inch-tall example, traced from a printed illustration, the creation of such portraits helped ease the periods of boredom characteristic of long whaling voyages.

148

America's naval and maritime exploits found full expression at the hands of hundreds of artists, many yet unidentified, around the world. From sketches of Baltimore Clipper privateers in the War of 1812 to vivid scenes of World War II engagements in the Pacific, artists have frozen moments of our naval history. Likewise, Chinese, French, and Italian painters with names like Lai Sung, Roux, and DeSimone have contributed to a better appreciation of the importance of America's foreign commerce by portraying vessels and commercial activity in ports from Asia to the Mediterranean.

Water's mesmerizing effect has long influenced artists. Seascape paintings, especially since the early nineteenth century, have reflected man's changing view of his relationship with nature. The sea has been portrayed as both beneficent provider and ruthless foe, a duality apparent even today to those who observe or work the waters.

The role of the marine artist from the seventeenth to the twentieth centuries, whether ship portraitist or painter of seascapes, is explored through the museum's extensive collection of paintings, drawings, and prints. Through this two-dimensional medium visitors can gain a better grasp of our complex maritime experience.

For millennia the sea has provided man a battleground in the quest for control of the wealth derived from mercantile activity. The rise of European nation-states with their overseas empires only heightened the stakes. The ensuing centuries of naval combat contributed in various ways to the development—and ultimately the independence—of the British colonies in America.

The story of western seapower is more than a tale of human weakness or failed diplomacy. There is another constant at work here—technological change. A major exhibit examines this phenomenon from the Age of the Galley to what we might call the

149
Portsmouth, New Hampshire, carver John H. Bellamy was already well-known for his decorative eagles when he created this 1¹/₂-ton masterpiece for the steam frigate USS Lancaster *in 1880–81. At a time when figureheads were becoming obsolete, Bellamy's massive eagle helped convey the sense of American power wherever the warship sailed.*

150
The Art Deco movement found expression afloat in the form of this stained and painted glass triptych from the smoking lounge of the United Fruit Co. steamer Veragua, *1932. Flanking the vessel's portrait are stylized depictions of the ports of New York and Havana.*

151

152

153

151
The mid-19th-century Luminist movement in American art found inspiration in both romantic landscapes and workaday scenes. In ''Gloucester Inner Harbor,'' by Fitz Hugh Lane (1804–65), soft light visually unifies the natural world and the manmade, implying a harmonious balance between the two.

152
Thirty-eight feet of gleaming mahogany, the 1929 Chris-Craft commuter-cruiser *Simokon* shares space with dozens of other power, rowing, and sailing craft. The story of recreational boating, from inexpensive canoes to luxury yachts, is vividly portrayed by watercraft like *Simokon*.

153
The 30-foot *Mariner*, first of several Chesapeake Bay ''deadrise'' workboats to be built at the museum, takes shape in 1980.

154
Philip Little's ''The Herring Dipper'' is a masterpiece of American impressionism. Painted ca. 1912, it reflected a growing interest among artists in capturing the local color of surviving maritime activities.

155
Often dismissed as overly sentimental, in fact, the work of John George Brown (1831–1913) went well beyond the portraits of city newsboys and street urchins for which he is best known. ''Grand Manan Fisherman,'' ca. 1878, illustrates Brown's ability to capture the strong play of light and shadow in a setting far from his normal urban haunts.

Age of the Aircraft Carrier. Basic evolutions in ship design and propulsion methods are two examples of change. Weaponry is yet another fundamental element in the equation. Examples of ordnance include a sixteenth-century crossbow called an "arbalest," a smooth-bore cannon from General Cornwallis's fleet at the battle of Yorktown, a Civil War-vintage Dahlgren gun, and the muzzle of a battleship's sixteen-inch naval rifle.

Chesapeake Bay is closely linked with America's naval past, primarily due to its strategic location. It has seen its share of piracy and privateering, and during the American Revolution it provided the stage for the decisive victory at Yorktown. Britain later turned this vital interior waterway into an invasion route during the War of 1812.

The American Civil War brought blockade and riverine warfare to the Bay and its streams. The area also witnessed an indecisive 1862 duel, now called the Battle of the Ironclads, between the Union's *Monitor* and the Confederacy's *Virginia* or *Merrimac*. Fought only a few miles from the site of the museum, the battle profoundly changed the future course of naval warfare. Appropriately, the museum has been named the national repository for the collection of *Monitor* artifacts and related material, and the largest item so far recovered, the ironclad's novel anchor, is on exhibit.

Modern naval history on the Bay has included pioneering developments in avia-

154 *155*

156

tion and amphibious warfare. Today the area is the birthplace of many warships and is home to the largest naval complex in the world.

The broader maritime history of Chesapeake Bay presents a vivid tapestry of peoples, ideas, and technological change. From tribal life to colonial settlement, and through industrialization to regional urban planning, the Bay has been the constant factor. Once important as both a protective barrier and vital highway, today the Bay serves as a provider of food and source of recreation. From Indian dugouts to nuclear-powered aircraft carriers, Chesapeake Bay has reflected the nature and pace of change in the world at large. To provide a penetrating glimpse into this phenomenon that surrounds and so profoundly affects the people along the Bay, the museum has completed a major gallery addition. Benefiting from the rich artifact and photographic holdings in the collection, and incorporating more interactive and ''hands-on'' features, this gallery brings to life the

156
The issue of safety afloat has never been taken lightly in seafaring cultures. English artist George Moreland (1763–1804) handled the subject dramatically in ''The Wreck of the Halsewell,'' *ca. 1786, based on the tragic loss of the British East Indiaman.*

complex, fascinating story of life on and along the Bay. Appropriately, the large fresnel lens from the Cape Charles lighthouse, which for so many years guided ships into the Bay, now towers high above the floor, guiding visitors into the exhibit.

The history of our maritime world is composed of more than large oceangoing vessels, major ports, and famous battles. It is in fact the sum total of the experiences of many hundreds of individual seafaring cultures, each with its own traditions, outlooks, and technologies. Perhaps no single class of artifact better represents many of these cultures than the types of small craft developed by each.

The international hue of The Mariners' Museum is most clearly evident in its extensive watercraft collection. Hailing from five continents, well over one hundred examples of small craft represent such basic functions as fishing, recreation, and lifesaving. A Welsh coracle, a round skin boat of ancient design, stands in contrast to a sleek,

157
''The San Francisco Coast,'' ca. 1872, captures the majestic topography and sky of the rugged California shoreline. Attributed to Albert Bierstadt (1830–1902), this work symbolizes the age old struggle between the works of man and the relentless power of nature. As the wreckage in the surf suggests, this contest often holds fatal consequences for man.

mahogany Chris-Craft express cruiser. *Dilemma*, Nathanael Herreshoff's pioneering fin-keel sloop of 1891, is juxtaposed with a Portuguese kelp boat and an experimental hydrofoil. This variety of form, function, and finish testifies to the kaleidoscopic nature of the world's maritime heritage.

Complementing such local watercraft examples in the museum as a crabbing skiff, Dodge Boat runabout, and sailing log canoe is an active program to preserve wooden boatbuilding skills. Through a cooperative program with local schools, interested young people and experienced boatbuilders join to construct traditional Chesapeake Bay craft, from sailing skipjacks to powered "deadrise" fishing and workboats. A spacious boatshop allows work to proceed in all weather and enables visitors to appreciate firsthand the transformation of lumber into a thing of functional beauty.

While artifacts provide the basic learning tools for most visitors, the museum also undertakes more specialized educational programs. From preschooler to graduate student, interested persons can find a wide variety of classroom and nonstructured programs addressing different facets of man's sea experience, both on the Bay and around the world.

Supporting the museum's exhibition and education programs is a superb reference library that, together with vast manuscript and photographic collections, attracts hundreds of researchers annually. Major specialized collections, like the Chris-Craft archives, draw many with very particular interests.

Despite the well-formed image of America as a nation closely bound to the land, history shows a strong orientation to the sea. This is an important component of the national identity, unique in many ways. But it is also a heritage that owes much to other, older traditions, including that of Native Americans. As a nation of seaborne immigrants America has benefited from nautical experience brought from many shores. The resulting mixture—always interesting, occasionally spicy—continues to evolve, subject now, as in the past, to the influence of the larger maritime world.

The tools of the museum's trade are many and varied: artifacts, manuscripts, still and moving film images, labels, and, most important, people. Add to these ingredients live demonstrations of music, woodcarving, boatbuilding, and sailors' handiwork. The result is a very special view of the maritime world, and a better understanding of America's place in it.

158
The work of James Bard (1815–97) has proved invaluable in documenting the appearance of hundreds of river and coastal vessels like the 1852 Hudson River towboat America. *Bard's undeniable draftsmanship, coupled with a wondrous sense of immediacy and detail, lends his portraits a special exuberance.*

L. Brainard, Commander

158

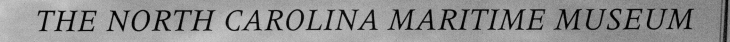

THE NORTH CAROLINA MARITIME MUSEUM

The North Carolina Maritime Museum

BEAUFORT · NORTH CAROLINA

Cape Hatteras. Cape Lookout. Cape Fear. Graveyard of the Atlantic. Names known to all mariners; names associated with storm and peril. Yet, for all the notoriety they bring, the stories behind these names are but a small part of North Carolina's maritime heritage.

Stretching southward from Cape Lookout, literally in the shadow of its historic lighthouse, is an unspoiled barrier island called Shackleford Banks. The bones of ships helplessly driven ashore by countless nameless storms lie buried beneath its beaches. The relentless surf, sometimes caressing, often thunderous, alternately exposes and obscures their skeletal remains.

Tucked peacefully behind this battered ribbon of dunes and sparse vegetation is the picturesque, historic town of Beaufort. Surveyed in 1713, it was incorporated in 1722, and is the third oldest town in the state. Although the bar at the inlet would not allow the largest sea-going vessels to enter the harbor, Beaufort was one of the three major ports through which the bulk of the colony's trade passed. Schooners and brigs loaded naval stores for England and New England, lumber products for the West Indies, and brought manufactured goods from England. Rum, molasses, salt, and fruit were among the imports from the islands.

Today, Beaufort's strategic location makes it the ideal starting point for cruising sailors headed offshore for the sunny Caribbean and other points south. It is also on the Intracoastal Waterway and sees much of that segment of the southern migration as well. At peak season as many as two hundred transient boats might seek shelter in the snug natural harbor during periods of bad weather.

Beaufort is home to the North Carolina Maritime Museum, a young but rapidly growing museum which has undertaken the rather large task of interpreting the state's complex involvement with maritime activities.

The abundance of water within the state's boundaries has been a crucial factor in

159
Preceding pages: *Beaufort's tranquil harbor*

160
Sextants and other 18th-century navigational instruments displayed on the desk of the Snap Dragon, *a noted 1812 privateer commanded by Captain Otway Burns*

160

161

its settlement and growth, both as a hindrance and a help. It has decidedly shaped lives in eastern North Carolina: one cannot go far on land without having to cross a body of water. On the other hand, the very universality of water makes it an ideal avenue for travel. From the very first inhabitants, to present-day coastal dwellers, boats have been a necessity.

For the visitor to the coast, the abundance and variety of natural resources such as woodlands, wildlife, and seafood and the beauty of the environment are immediately absorbed. It was so even for the first English explorers; in 1584 Arthur Barlowe reported in glowing terms the bounty of the new land that would become North Carolina: "The soile is the most plentifull, sweete, fruitfull, and wholsome of all the world. . . ." A year later Ralph Lane, governor of the first experimental English colony, described mainland North Carolina as the "goodliest soile under the cope of heaven, so abounding with sweete trees. . . ." A subsequent attempt at colonization would fail but would bequeath to the world the romantic mystery of the "Lost Colony" and the first child of English parents to be born in the new land.

As part of the state's celebration of the four-hundredth anniversary of those first

161
Portsmouth Island Lifesaving Station in the late 19th century. Its location near Ocracoke Inlet and Diamond Shoals kept crews alert and busy until the service was replaced by the U.S. Coast Guard.

efforts to plant a colony in America, the North Carolina Maritime Museum undertook research to discover what kind of small boats were used in the early English explorations. The result was a full-scale reconstruction of a 24-foot ship's boat, designed and built at the museum, and now used in reenactments and other programs that afford a glimpse of what travel was like in sixteenth-century Carolina.

The research and documentation of small craft is a major emphasis of the museum. The variety of local conditions and the diversity of uses for the water gave rise to a number of indigenous boat types. Broad sounds, protected bays, wide rivers, and narrow, winding creeks share at least one common characteristic; the water is spread very thin. Even the relatively deeper sounds are dotted with sandbars and ''oyster rocks'' that make the navigation of deep-drafted vessels impossible or, at best, extremely troublesome.

In the 1870s an expanding population and industrial developments created new markets for seafood and fish products. Boatbuilding, fishing, and seafood processing burgeoned throughout coastal North Carolina. Boatbuilders in diverse communities skillfully devised boats ideally suited to their needs and localities. The somewhat deeper

162
Sharpies like this were very common around Beaufort in the last quarter of the 19th century. Here, the boat that provides much of the family income also serves for a Sunday outing.

waters of the north and central portions of the coast permitted the use of round-bottom and V-bottom boat types more suitable for coping with the bigger seas and violent summer squalls that arose with alarming frequency. In the southern sections, shallow V- and flat-bottom boat types prevailed.

The round-bottom shad boat, or seine boat, was a popular style born on the shores of Roanoke Island, scene of the "Lost Colony." Used for fishing pound nets and for other utilitarian chores, this boat had a reputation among local fishermen for speed and sea-worthiness.

Originally built as sailing boats, many were converted to power in the early 1900s. A few still operate on the central sounds. More lie discarded in out-of-the-way places; still more live in the memories of old sailors and in the tales they spin. In one such story, two sailors are in their shad boat working nets in a blistering spring gale. One says to the other, "Look to loo'ard and tell me how many boats you see, Bill!" "Cap'n Tom, there ain't any boats. Only steamships, and they're looking for harbor!" is Bill's reply. Another tale, extolling the ability of shad boats to sail to windward, nevertheless stretches the truth a bit by claiming that a certain builder's boats would sail "so close to the wind that they never had to tack."

The humor of hard-working people often deals with the hardships they face in day-to-day tasks. The small craft they use reflect the nature of their work as well as the

163
The main building of the North Carolina Maritime Museum is an all-wood structure that has traditional Beaufort accents blended with architectural elements from the 19th-century U.S. Lifesaving Stations that once dotted the North Carolina coast.

165

164

economics and technology of their times. For those and other reasons, it is prudent to preserve the boats as primary evidence of life in another time.

The sharpie was the "mule" of the sounds and creeks. It was a tough, inexpensive, adaptable workboat. This swift-sailing, flat-bottomed New Englander was brought to Beaufort in 1874, where it out-sailed the local boats rather impressively. Such was their immediate acceptance that in just five years there were over five hundred sharpies in the area, most of them locally built. Modifications to meet specific local conditions and uses resulted in a distinct type of sharpie known as the Core Sound Sharpie. Larger and more powerful than its predecessor, it was used for oyster dredging as well as freight and produce hauling. These modifications also made the boats more suitable for coastwise voyaging and many undertook trading voyages to the West Indies during the summer, a surprising feat of navigation for a vessel of flat-bottom construction.

Oystering has been an important commercial activity since the middle of the nineteenth century. It was an important food even earlier. North Carolina waters have been major producers, but resources are not inexhaustible. The heavy demand for oysters and other shellfish brought about an urgent need to regulate harvesting to ensure an ample supply of shellfish for the growing market. Thus, an active research program has yielded much information about the biology of coastal marine life and has given us new insight into the importance of the marsh-fringed bodies of water lying between seashore

164
Fine woodwork and tasteful furnishings distinguish the museum's reference library. There is a wide range of volumes on maritime history, boatbuilding, historical vessels, navigation and cruising, marine biology, and natural history, as well as specialty pieces such as a rare, 1694 Dutch book on shipbuilding.

165
North Carolina decoys from the James Lewis Collection. The head of the brant (top left) is made from a natural root shape, for durability. It is turn-of-the-century and comes from Portsmouth Island. The canvasback drake (bottom) was made ca. 1875 by Ned Burgess, noted decoy maker from Waterlilly. The red drake (top right) is from Church's Island.

and mainland. Estuaries, as they are called, are habitats vital for the growth and survival of many important species. The natural history of the oyster illustrates the delicate balance between biology and habitat common to many important marine species.

In its first couple of weeks of life, the oyster is a free-floating larva at the mercy of currents, predators, and other hazards. At a crucial point in its development it must find a hard surface on which to attach itself for further growth. Only the marshes, tidal creeks, bays, and sounds provide these conditions for what we now perceive as "nurseries of the sea."

Shellfish beds play still another role in the estuary environment. They are hosts to complex communities of organisms that in turn furnish a food supply for fish and other "swimmers." Some of these, like drum, weakfish, crabs, and shrimp, are also subject to commercial harvest.

An intricacy of patterns emerges as our knowledge becomes more complete, patterns that weave together the environment, the organisms, and man in an inseparable web, each dependent upon the other.

Man, in a manner of speaking, sits atop these patterns. As primary beneficiary of nature's bounty, he alone among the species bears the weight of stewardship. This interrelationship of human activities with the coastal environment is the theme upon which the museum bases most of its exhibits, programs, and publications.

The museum's collections attempt to further delineate this history of hearty, resourceful fisherman-farmers, eking out a livelihood in remote waterfront villages,

166
Model of a Core Sound workboat. The boat's lines clearly show its sharpie heritage. The "dog house," forward, was a foul weather steering station.

167
Plank and frame model of the 1775 brig Lexington, *made in the 1960s by former museum modeler Lt. Cmdr. John S. MacCormack, USCG Ret.*

166   167

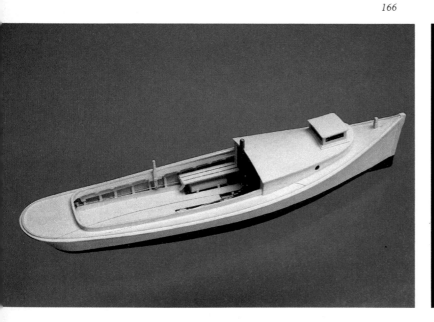

168
*Adze, slicks, planes and adjustable
bevel from the collection of 19th-
century shipwright's tools*

169
*Part of the collection of 26 scrimshaw
pieces made with whales' teeth and
ivory by Lt. Cmdr. MacCormack in the
1960s and 1970s*

170
*Buoy net needles, net mesh gages, and
trout sounder typify the waterman's
self-reliance. The trout sounder is a
clever device used to remove the sound
or air bladder through the gill opening
without cutting open the fish. Trout
sound was once a marketable delicacy.*

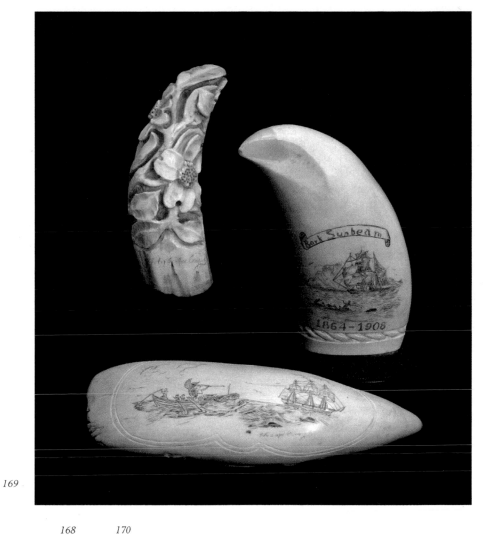

169

168   170

sometimes in harmony, often in seeming conflict, with timeless natural order and processes.

It isn't very different today. Of course there are now telephones, automobiles, paved roads, and bridges connecting communities on opposite shores. But the people retain their strong, independent nature, and live close to the land and water—the earth— building their own skiffs from native woods and making much of their own fishing gear. Many still farm to supplement their existence, and most now take jobs in town and do their fishing at night.

Their boats illustrate adaptability; flaring bows and broad beams accommodate powerful engines which enable part-time watermen to speed to the fishing grounds and return with their catches. Less time spent in one undertaking means more time for another. Rapid mobility also means that the weather is a lesser factor, since the modern sailor need not forecast bad weather so much in advance. If a summer squall is spotted on the horizon, there is time enough for the modern power boat to find shelter.

In former times, the savvy coastal dweller read the coming weather by observing wind speed and direction, changes in temperature and barometric pressure, and signs in the skies—the clouds. Fishing was always undertaken with due regard for weather and the tides.

A north wind blowing over cold water makes very harsh conditions in which to work. Both oystering and wildfowling were winter occupations on the Carolina sounds. After 1916, when professional hunting was banned by federal law, some of the "pro's" turned to guiding sport hunters to ease the loss of income.

Guns, boats, and decoys made up the special equipment of the hunter. The use of sink boxes, or "batteries" as they were called, obviated the development of specialized boats for gunning, such as were used on Chesapeake Bay, Delaware Bay, and elsewhere. The gunner lies flat in a battery, which is weighted down to float low in the water, and waits for ducks or geese to be fooled by decoys into landing nearby.

The decoys were carved from wood or shaped from other materials by hand. They are considered collectible folk art and often command a high price, depending on age, condition, carver, and species.

Among the many waterfowl decoys at North Carolina Maritime Museum is a collection made by the late James S. Lewis, Jr., who was once known as the state's "dean of decoy collectors." The collection comprises 112 "birds," many of which are rare and extremely valuable, and illustrates the range of styles and materials used by North Carolina decoy makers. Mr. Lewis was a noted civil engineer and avid duck hunter who wrote, "The time may come when the old duck hunter is content to put his gun away, throw the patched-up waders in the garbage can, and reflect in comfort on occurrences which could be considered pleasant only in retrospect. . . . However, it may turn out that

171
The museum staff spent eighteen months in the research, design, and construction of a reproduction of a 16th-century vessel known as the 1584 ship's boat. The project typifies the museum's versatility and emphasis on research and watercraft.

172

173

memories are not an adequate substitute for the excitement and punishment which are part of waterfowl hunting. . . ." His remarkable collection of decoys may have gone far in redressing this lack.

Ducks, geese, swans, and other species using the Atlantic Flyway still winter in large numbers on the lakes and sounds in North Carolina. In fact, high year-round populations of both seasonal and resident species reflect the quality and variety of natural habitat. Barrier and spoil islands provide nesting areas for terns, skimmers, and other shore birds, and woodland sites harbor a host of songbirds.

It may not be so obvious that coastal woodlands are considered within the maritime realm. However, in terms of geological and biological relationships, there is an undeniable link. Swamps and vast peat bogs, known as pocosins, occupy ancient estuaries. Pine savannahs lie on prehistoric dunes and sea beaches. The characteristics of these older geological features determine the kind of plant community the site will support.

The tree of the savannahs is the long leaf pine. It thrives there because it is resistant to fire, a common natural occurrence during dry periods, and it tolerates the extreme conditions of wet and dry to which the sand ridges are subject.

In earlier times the long leaf was important commercially as a source of turpentine and pitch—naval stores. It was also in demand for its timber. Long, straight boles made

172
Where once upon a time sleek, white, working watercraft vied with the elements to produce unique coastal lifestyles, an endless variety of small pleasure craft provides diversion from workday pressures for modern day sailors.

173
The museum's annual traditional wooden boat show is an educational program that promotes the aesthetic and functional values of small wooden boats and features displays and lots of action on the water.

174
The reproduction of the 1584 ship's boat under sail. Operated as a living exhibit and training vessel, it was built at the museum for the Elizabeth II State Historic Site in Manteo, North Carolina.

174

good ship's masts, and the dense, rot-resistant wood was excellent for keels, decks, and hull planking. Its resin content also made it disagreeable to teredos—ship worms—and therefore ideal for ship construction.

Near the edges of these pine savannahs, where they border the wetter shrub thickets, is the habitat of one of the jewels of the plant world: the tiny, secretive, and rare Venus flytrap. This fascinating little plant has leaves that work like baited, hinged traps to lure and ensnare luckless insects attracted by their red coloring and sweet-smelling nectar.

This is a little of what the North Carolina Maritime Museum is about. From the offshore storms and deep-sea creatures to the woodlands and streams of the coastal plain, and all in between.

It is to this "in between"—where the people and the environment have melded together in unique relationships; where land and water intermingle and "marry"; where maritime "crawls out" on land and land takes to the water—that the museum finds its most important calling. It is a land of incredible beauty, unbelievably rich in wildlife and natural resources. But its tranquility is deceptive. Development, both commercial and industrial; the press of expanding population; the flooding tide of tourism, recreational homes, and time-sharing condominiums; all innocently and quite unintentionally pose serious threats to the future of much of what we find desirable and attractive about the coast. Only research and education hold the key to the peaceful coexistence of opposing factors. Knowledge of our maritime heritage, of environmental mechanisms, and awareness of the beauty and intricacy of our world will help preserve this precious legacy.

The patterns, the interdependencies, the natural as well as the cultural communities are all explored in museum field trips and programs that are designed to put fun into learning. The traditional skills of the boatbuilders, their boats, tools, and glimpses into their lives are part of the museum's offering. Lighthouses, U.S. Lifesaving Service, sailors' arts, ship models. Shipwrecks, weather, and navigation. Ports and shipping. Fishing, fishing gear, and even the fish.

The list could go on and on. Maritime and North Carolina. It's a story worth knowing.

175
Field trips to mud flats, marshes, barrier islands and maritime forests turn learning into adventure for both young and adult participants.

175

THE MANITOWOC MARITIME MUSEUM

The Manitowoc Maritime Museum

MANITOWOC · WISCONSIN

In 1851, William Bates, a shipwright who had just arrived in Wisconsin from Maine, suggested that "we call Manitowoc the 'Clipper City' and then name the vessel I was building for it." His idea was immediately accepted, and over the next century Manitowoc was unofficially known as "Clipper City." It became synonymous with shipbuilding and transportation on the Great Lakes.

Today, much of that legacy and heritage is preserved by the Manitowoc Maritime Museum. Ironically, however, it was neither the wooden clipper nor the iron steamer that served as the catalyst for the creation of this museum; rather it was the construction of steel submarines for the U.S. Navy that precipitated the museum's founding.

In September 1940, the Navy awarded a construction contract to the Manitowoc Shipbuilding Company for ten submarines. Within five years 28 submarines had been built. Of the 28, 25 saw action in World War II and made their way from Manitowoc through the Chicago River and Sanitary Canal to Lockport, Illinois. Then they were transported aboard a floating drydock down the Illinois and Mississippi rivers to the Gulf of Mexico.

By the mid-1960s, local longing for a Manitowoc submarine to return permanently to her home port had crystallized. A Submarine Memorial Association was incorporated on January 11, 1968, with James Gogats elected its first president. The search for an available Manitowoc submarine quickened. An offer by the U.S. Navy of the USS *Redfin*, the eighth submarine built in Manitowoc, was declined because of the extensive alterations which had been done to the boat following World War II. Agreement, however, was finally reached with the Navy for another vessel, and with much fanfare the USS *Cobia* arrived in Manitowoc on August 17, 1970, to become the principal exhibit of the Manitowoc Maritime Museum.

Citing Manitowoc and her growth as a typical example of port development on the

176
Preceding pages: *The USS* Cobia, *moored adjacent to the museum, recreates a scene from half a century ago when submarines regularly passed through the Manitowoc River for sea trials in Lake Michigan.*

177
Richard Young, one of the foremost modelers in the Midwest and a regular museum volunteer, at work on White Swan, *an 85-foot freighter built by the Burger Boat Co. in 1925. Eleven of Young's models line the museum's Maritime Arts and Crafts Gallery.*

177

178

179

Great Lakes, the Maritime Museum established itself as a strong regional resource, celebrating the commerce and transportation on the Inland Seas.

The maritime traditions of the Great Lakes differ somewhat from their coastal and transoceanic counterparts. The earliest commercial use of sail in the Great Lakes region grew from the advantage in both time and increased carrying capacity that could be achieved by using inland waters instead of primitive overland routes. The railroad did not reach portions of the upper Midwest until the 1870s, and roads were poor and offered limited transportation capabilities. Grain and other products of the Midwest could easily reach the population centers of the East by water, and the ships could then return swiftly with westward-moving immigrants, finished goods, and industrial products through the Great Lakes and their tributaries and canals. Even in the twentieth century, transportation

178
Richard Young's model of Michigan, *a packet liner that operated between Buffalo and Detroit, took approximately 4,000 hours to complete and is regarded as one of his finest efforts.*

179
The hull section of the Clipper City, *built to full scale with a beam of 27 feet 6 inches, is based on William Bates's original mold-loft notebook, the earliest found to date on the Great Lakes. Sixteen illustrations by noted marine artist Sam Manning detail the step-by-step construction of a schooner.*

across the Lakes offers savings of time and money when compared to traversing the circuitous overland routes.

When shipwright William Bates, apparently a disciple of John W. Griffiths, the noted East Coast designer and builder, arrived in Manitowoc in those early days, he brought to the Lakes the concept of scientific ship construction. For over twelve years his yard produced some of the finest sailing vessels on the Lakes. Rigged with fore-and-aft sails, schooners became the dominant vessel on the Great Lakes until the advent of iron ships. Today, one can view a reproduction of Bates's handiwork in the Manitowoc Maritime Museum.

A cross-section replica of the *Clipper City* anchors the Wooden Ship portion of the permanent exhibit hall and illustrates the same wooden ship construction methods used

180
Juxtaposed against the Clipper City, *the recreated lakefront buildings emphasize the historical relationships among agriculture, industry, commerce, and transportation on the Great Lakes.*

by Bates and his contemporaries. The original ship, built in Manitowoc in 1854, incorporated a clipper bow, a shallow draft, a centerboard, and sharp ends underwater. This design provided speed, maneuverability, and expanded cargo capacity and was a revolutionary advance for Great Lakes vessels. Similarly, exhibiting a full-scale cross-section of a wooden vessel was a revolutionary step for maritime museums and represents one of the most complete efforts in any gallery to display the techniques of nineteenth-century wooden shipbuilding.

Near the *Clipper City* can be seen a re-created portion of Manitowoc's harbor front. Full-size buildings rise to heights of twenty-four feet, transporting visitors back to a boom period of regional growth. Two of the storefronts interpret the Great Lakes' contribution to regional agriculture. William Rahr's Sons, a local malting concern founded in 1847 by William Rahr as a brewery and malthouse, boasted in 1909 that three-fourths of the brewers in America used Rahr's patent caramel malt from Manitowoc. Next to Rahr's building stands the Albert Landreth Company.

Albert Landreth began experimenting with canning vegetables in 1883 and, four years later, founded the Albert Landreth Company on the Manitowoc lakefront, the first commercial cannery in Wisconsin. A full selection of early Landreth canned goods, all bearing period labels reproduced expressly for this exhibit by Lakeside Packing Company, the successor of Landreth's company, adorns the shelves of the building.

One of the reasons for Landreth's success was his use of car-ferry service. Prior to the 1892 launching of the wooden car ferry *Ann Arbor No. 1*, all railroad cargo crossing Lake Michigan was removed from railcars, placed into steamers for the Lake voyage, and then reloaded onto railcars on the opposite shores. The car ferry accommodated railcars and provided an alternative to this time-consuming and costly process. The *City of Midland No. 41* is the last operating vestige of what once was the largest car-ferry fleet in the world. A scale model of this vessel, along with the pristine capstan from the *Pere Marquette No. 19*, one of the early car ferries, can also be seen.

The remaining gallery buildings played daily roles in Lake transportation. The Rand and Roemer Hardware Company was one of several chandleries that flourished in Manitowoc. This re-created building shows a myriad assortment of ropes, navigational instruments, blocks, chains, lifesaving supplies, wire, and other naval supplies necessary to outfit and maintain sailing and steam vessels on the Lakes.

One company which undoubtedly frequented Rand and Roemer Hardware was the Goodrich Transportation Company. A re-created baggage and ticket office, highlighting the line's dual cargoes of passengers and freight, completes the gallery waterfront. Founded in 1856 by Captain Albert E. Goodrich, Goodrich Transportation became the largest, most prosperous, and longest-lived steamboat company on the Great Lakes. Shortly after the line's founding, it forged a lasting relationship with Manitowoc. Nine-

181
The USS Pogy *(SS266) was side-launched at Manitowoc Shipbuilding Co. on June 23, 1942. The* Pogy *was the second submarine launched at Manitowoc and the first submarine launched with machinery inside.*

181

teen steamships were built here for Goodrich during a fifty-six-year period; Manitowoc also served as port-of-hail for the line from 1868 to 1881.

A scale model of Goodrich's *Sheboygan*, an 1869 side-wheel steamer built by G. S. Rand of Manitowoc, shows the typical steamer prominent on the Lakes until the 1880s. Side-wheel steamers like the *Sheboygan* brought farmers and immigrants who settled the Midwest to their new homes, and also carried mail, excursionists, and package goods.

Artifacts from the *Christopher Columbus*, another legendary Goodrich vessel, a scale model of the ship, and decorative panels and furnishings from its interior document the popularity of this sole whaleback passenger ship. Designed with a unique cigar-shaped hull, she carried five thousand passengers per trip from downtown Chicago to the 1893 Columbian Exposition. In her first year of service, the *Christopher Columbus* transported over two million passengers. Active in the Goodrich Line until 1932, she earned the distinction of carrying more passengers than any other Great Lakes vessel before she was scrapped in Manitowoc.

Unfortunately, other Goodrich vessels met with a similar demise in Manitowoc. Many of the nameboards from these and other vessels, however, have been preserved in the museum. In fact, Edwin Schuette, a local maritime enthusiast and collector, assembled over fifty nameboards as both wooden and steel vessels were repaired, remodeled, or scrapped in Manitowoc shipyards. His collecting efforts helped preserve an extremely sentimental segment of regional maritime lore.

Schuette also participated in the formation of another important regional collection through his collaboration with Captain Edward Carus of Manitowoc. Together, they assembled one of the most comprehensive collections of photographs and memorabilia on the wooden-shipbuilding era of the Great Lakes.

Carus began his career as a salt boy in the Manitowoc shipyards after the Civil War. In 1874, at age fourteen, he shipped aboard the schooner *Luna* and began an association with the Lakes and Lake history that would last until his death in 1947. Throughout his fifty-seven-year career, he collected over three thousand photographs, dating from the 1860s to the 1930s, compiled one of the earliest lists of shipwrecks on the Lakes, assembled extensive memorabilia from the Goodrich Line and other companies, including original logs, ship models, and half models, and generally gathered and preserved a unique and irreplaceable body of material. Carus was one of the earliest Great Lakes' marine historians. Recognizing the importance of sharing his collection with others, he opened a local marine museum whose artifacts would ultimately be merged with those of James Gogats's Submarine Memorial Association.

In a 1938 letter to a friend, Carus wrote, "We have the best marine museum on the Lakes which strangers should not miss. . . ." In a subsequent postcard, written after his wife's illness had led him to part with his collection, he lamented, "I sold my whole damn

182
The schooner Lizzie Metzner *was built in Manitowoc by Rand and Burger in 1888 for Mashek and Metzner of Kewaunee, Wisconsin. Used primarily for hauling lumber, the* Metzner *is shown at dock near the lumber yard in Manitowoc in 1898.*

183
Captain Edward Carus (far right) began his 57-year career on the lakes at the age of 14. From 1892 to 1903 he was a captain for the prestigious Goodrich Transportation Co.

182

183

Yarn Spinners.

1907

184

185

marine collection, anchor stock, martin-gale, rudder, centerboard, and galley stove. I am now a mere landlubber, am now taking up court etiquette and del sarte [sic]. Tell Mr. McDonald and the rest of your friends if they come here to see a marine collection they will be disappointed." Fortunately, disappointment and obscurity were not the end of Carus's collection, as his entire archive returned home to Manitowoc some forty years later.

The 1938 sale of material had been transacted with Mr. Henry N. Barkhausen of Chicago. Barkhausen was interested in establishing a maritime museum in Chicago, but this never came to pass. Instead he retained the material until he donated the complete collection to the Maritime Museum in December 1980, together with additional items.

Carus's years on the Lakes touched two centuries and witnessed many advances in maritime transportation. Perhaps none of those advances is more awesome, however, than the evolution of the bulk freighter. Designed to transport natural resources of the Midwest to refining and production facilities around the Great Lakes, these workhorses gradually grew from an early capacity of 1,000 tons to nearly 70,000 tons. Within the gallery one finds several scale models which clearly illustrate this development. Both the *Charles W. Wetmore*, an 1891 whaleback freighter, and the *American Republic*, a 634-foot loop-belt self-unloader built in 1980–81, demonstrate these amazing technological and shipbuilding innovations. Also on view is a 5-by-12-foot section cut from the keel of the *Frontenac*, a 600-foot steam freighter built in 1923. Rivets, flanges, and webs of the keel section are exposed for total inspection. They impart an idea of the massiveness of these ships and provide a unique look at steel ship construction techniques.

Many of these techniques were employed by Manitowoc Shipbuilding Company. Founded in 1902 as the Manitowoc Dry Dock Company, the yard established a reputation as one of the finest construction facilities on the Great Lakes. Seventy metal ships were launched between 1902 and 1916. This effort was intensified during World War I when thirty-three ocean freighters were built. This war expansion program transformed Manitowoc Shipbuilding Company into one of the largest and most modern shipyards on the Great Lakes.

Because of its position as a regional leader, it was natural for Manitowoc Shipbuilding to pioneer welding methods on the Great Lakes. By 1937, the yard was producing vessels that were nearly all welded. This capability was perfected just in time for the yard's entry into the effort for World War II.

In September 1940, Manitowoc Shipbuilding Company began work on ten submarines. The first, USS *Peto*, was completed 288 days ahead of schedule and contracts for forty-seven additional submarines eventually followed. Of the twenty-eight submarines actually built, twenty-five served in the Pacific theater, and four, the USS *Golet, Kete, Largato,* and *Robalo*, were lost at sea. Numerous engineering and production problems

184
The whaleback passenger vessel Christopher Columbus *was built in 1892 in Superior, Wisconsin. The only one of her kind, the* Columbus *made her last voyage in 1932.*

185
The Chicago *was a side-wheel passenger steamer built in Manitowoc in 1873–74. The passenger vessel operated for the Goodrich Transportation Co. until 1915 and was dismantled in 1916.*

which Manitowoc Shipbuilding encountered and conquered are detailed in the exhibit, including the first side launching of a submarine.

This little-known, yet fascinating, chapter of naval history is explained in *Fresh Water Submarines: The Manitowoc Story*. Written by Rear Admiral William T. Nelson, USN (ret.), the commissioning-commanding officer of the USS *Peto*, this book chronicles the first Manitowoc submarine from its construction until its arrival in the Pacific theater.

A guided tour aboard the USS *Cobia* realistically re-creates the atmosphere of those times. Although built by the Electric Boat Company in Groton, Connecticut, the *Cobia* was an identical sister ship of the twenty-eight submarines built by Manitowoc Shipbuilding. Her outstanding war record included six patrols during which she rescued seven downed American pilots and sank thirteen Japanese vessels to account for 18,000 tons of enemy shipping. This record, coupled with her physical integrity, appearance, and interpretive visitor program, led the U.S. Department of the Interior to declare her a National Historic Landmark on January 14, 1986.

Another local yard involved with World War II vessel construction was the Burger Boat Company, Inc. Established in the 1890s, the yard's expertise in wooden construction techniques proved invaluable during World War II. Fourteen minesweepers, eight wooden subchasers, and other wooden and steel vessels were built by Burger for the U.S. Navy. But Burger's most noted contribution to regional maritime history was and still is its yacht construction. Experiments with steel hull fabrication in the 1920s led Burger in 1938 to build the first steel-welded yacht in the United States. This innovation was followed by the first flush deck cruiser just prior to World War II, and the first all-aluminum hull in 1954. This innovative spirit has, on several occasions, led the Burger yard to break its own world records for vessel size and construction techniques.

The Manitowoc Maritime Museum celebrates these preeminent shipbuilders and the vessels they constructed. Its collection of memorabilia assembled by Schuette, Carus, Gogats, and others, along with its re-creation of waterfront businesses, round out its presentation of man's use of his nautical environment. The skill, tenacity, and ingenuity which led shipwrights in the nineteenth century to work through the dead of Wisconsin winters in the construction of schooners, and which, one hundred years later, inspired women, farmers, and other nontraditional workers to become overnight welders, riveters, and pipe fitters for the production of submarines, lives today in the Manitowoc Maritime Museum. The emergence of the museum from inception in 1968 to regional leader in less than twenty years is a tribute not only to the history it preserves, but to the foresight, dedication, and community spirit which would not allow a treasured legacy to be lost.

186
The Maritime Arts and Crafts Gallery features (left foreground) *the* Alabama, *built by Manitowoc Shipbuilding Co. in 1909–10 for Goodrich Transportation Co., and* (right foreground) *the* Sally Ann, *a 3-masted ship model by Captain Thomas Olson.*

THE WOODWARD RIVERBOAT MUSEUM

11 Rafts, Steamboats, and the Lore of the Mississippi

Jerome Enzler, Director,
and Roger R. Osborne, Curator

The Woodward Riverboat Museum

DUBUQUE · IOWA

I am the Father of Waters, the Mississippi River. Wars of conquest and independence
were fought on my banks and thousands of immigrants have settled my shores.
I am the river that allowed the grandeur of the steamboat and the might of modern
transportation. When my surging waters overflow my banks, I flood the land that tries
to contain me. I am not contained. . . . I am the Mississippi.

This personification of the Mississippi River leads the visitor into the diverse and captivating exhibits of the Woodward Riverboat Museum. Located in Dubuque, Iowa, on the banks of the Mississippi, the museum tells the story of the river as it journeys through the five states of Minnesota, Wisconsin, Iowa, Illinois, and Missouri—stories of Indians and fur traders, lead miners, loggers, steamboat pilots, fishermen, pleasure boaters—"river people."

The recorded history of the "Misi Sipi," the Father of Waters, began when Louis Jolliet, Father Jacques Marquette, and five voyageurs explored the Great River in 1673. Entering the Mississippi from the Wisconsin River, the explorers encountered giant sturgeon that rammed the sides of their birchbark canoes. They found footprints on the sandy shore, leading them to their first contact with natives of the Mississippi River, the Peoria Indians. Going on, they saw the majestic pictographs of the Piasa birds painted on the side of a bluff near present Alton, Illinois. They negotiated a giant whirlpool and then the rush of the Missouri River as it joined the Mississippi above present St. Louis.

On the tricentennial of Jolliet and Marquette's expedition, their historic trip was reenacted in a national commemoration. One of the two canoes was given to the museum, along with the equipment used in the expedition, for use in a life-size depiction of the exploration of the Mississippi.

187
Preceding pages: *The side-wheel*
steamboat William M. Black, *built*
in 1934

188
The Clyde *was first iron-hulled*
steamboat on the Upper Mississippi.
She was built by the Iowa Iron Works
in 1870.

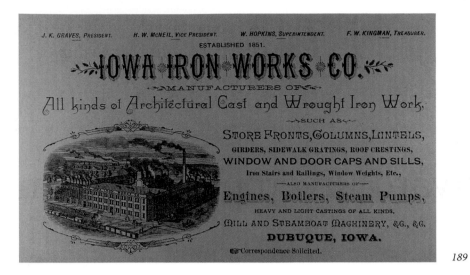

189

190

191

189
*Iowa Iron Works advertisement,
ca. 1886*

190
Torpedo boat Ericsson *in Dubuque Ice
Harbor, ca. 1895*

191
*Boatyard workers and beer bucket in a
boatbuilding exhibit of the Woodward
Riverboat Museum*

Sometimes the research techniques an institution employs are as wild as the subjects they are investigating—in this instance, the Mississippi River itself. One morning, to the puzzlement of the director, the exhibit team took the Jolliet and Marquette canoe out on the river. They were measuring the draft and photographing the wave pattern of the canoe as it was paddled through the water. These wave patterns were then accurately reproduced in a life-size diorama.

Although Marquette's journals have given him prominence, Jolliet was the true leader of the expedition, but his journals and maps were lost when his canoe capsized on the return voyage just two hours from Montreal. To finance the trip and hire five voyageurs, Jolliet was given a trading license to barter with the Indians. He was later surprised to learn, contrary to his expectation, that he had not borrowed his sister-in-law's canoe: upon coming home, she presented him with a bill for two years' rental of the birchbark canoe.

From northern Minnesota to Cairo, Illinois, the upper Mississippi River follows a winding course of some 1,260 miles, forming borders between Minnesota, Wisconsin, Iowa, Illinois, and Missouri. Fur traders were attracted to the rich shores and the river brought first French, and later English and American, traders. Soon the Indian abandoned his hunting and gathering ways and became a professional trapper, working each winter to gather furs which could be traded for iron, brass, and silver goods. Iron axes replaced stone celts, metal arrow- and spearheads replaced flint points, and Venetian beads and silver crosses became Indian foofaraw, along with shiny mirrors, ribbons, bells, and other ornaments.

Most of the museum's collection of Native American artifacts and trade-era goods comes from a privately-owned repository founded by a German immigrant, Richard Herrmann. From the 1880s to 1920s, Herrmann collected thousands of artifacts, and he searched and traded for the rest. A riverman retrieved an iron pipe tomahawk with inlaid silver and wooden handle/pipestem from the bottom of the Mississippi. Another gave Herrmann a dugout canoe, which he had purchased in the 1860s for fifty cents when a flotilla of Indian-made dugouts was brought downriver to Dubuque.

Effigy mounds dot the bluffs overlooking the Mississippi, and effigy pipes and bowls in the collection attest to the mystical beliefs of these first American rivermen. Copper and stone fish hooks and stone sinkers for nets represent the more practical side of Indian life, as do hundreds of stone bowls, axes, celts, and flint points collected along the river.

Along with the furs, the traders came for the lead ore. Before 1700, maps in Paris and London noted "mines de plumb," or lead mines, at Dubuque. Lead trading and mining posts were established in 1690, 1700, and 1741.

During the summer of 1778, the upper Mississippi River Valley was thrust into the

American Revolution. American troops led by George Rogers Clark captured British-controlled towns along the river in Illinois country. The following year, Spain, which controlled the lead mines that supplied vital ammunition, allied itself with Clark's troops and declared war with England. In response, the British devised an elaborate plan to gain control of the entire Mississippi. As forces from Detroit marched south to draw Clark away from the river, British troops located north of Dubuque and in Florida were to converge on St. Louis. The northern army of 300 British and 700 Indians captured the Dubuque lead mines, taking 17 prisoners and 60 tons of lead ore. They then proceeded downriver to St. Louis, but advance parties beat them there to warn of their approach. The Spanish, however, defeated the British in Florida, and without the element of surprise, the northern force was easily repulsed by the Spanish garrison at St. Louis.

After the war, French Canadian Julien Dubuque established himself at the lead mines, keeping several pirogues and canoes at his disposal for traveling the Mississippi and its tributaries. To appease the king of Spain, who controlled the lands west of the Mississippi, he named his lands the "Mines of Spain."

In the 1830s, Dubuque and nearby Galena, Illinois, were mining boom towns, their populations consisting of several thousand men and a couple of hundred women. The settlement of the upper Mississippi Valley lead mines was the first major mining rush in the history of the United States, predating the California gold rush by a quarter of a century. By the 1840s, Dubuque, Galena, and the surrounding cities on either side of the Mississippi River were producing 90 percent of the country's lead, 10 percent of the world's supply. The lead was used for bullets, shot and cannon balls, and also for the manufacture of paint. These yeomen of lead raised their "pigs," the name given to the pure lead ingots poured at the lead smelting furnace. "Get the lead out!" was the cry, and the keelboats and steamboats provided the transportation to do it. The boats brought the lead pigs downriver, returning with mining tools, dry goods, stoves, and farming equipment.

Dubuque is honeycombed with lead mines and caves, many still filled with the underground rails, carts, and pickaxes of the miners. The museum uses artifacts such as these in a replicated walk through a lead mine, replete with a lead miner, a windlass, and lead bucket overhead. Adjacent displays show the pig molds, the blasting powder spoons, a lead miner's money belt, and the pig tails, iron hooks that held the buckets onto the windlass rope allowing quick release. Like the mines, the river gives up its ghosts in the form of artifacts from the bottom such as an iron keelboat cannon used to protect lead cargo and to signal other boats.

In the early nineteenth century, a new type of vessel appeared on the Mississippi. The Indians saw the steamboat as an omen, a fire-eating dragon that belched smoke. And no wonder, for in 1811, the same year that the steamboat appeared on the Mississippi, the

192
Interior of the restored Aquila *pilothouse*

193
Replica of a lead mine, with mining artifacts

192

193

New Madrid earthquake shook the Midwest, tumbling huge sections of shore into the water and causing the Mississippi to flow backwards for a time.

Within a few years, the true Mississippi River steamboat evolved—a shallow draft vessel of four to five feet for shoal waters, with high-pressure engines to combat the swift currents and a wedding-cake tier of decks above the waterline. The main deck held the engines, cordwood, and freight, which could include livestock, circus animals, cast-iron stoves, and farmers' plows. Deck passengers who couldn't afford accommodations above slept with the livestock. Just above, the boiler deck had a row of staterooms on each side, each one named after a different state in the Union. The central corridor between the two rows of staterooms held the saloon, with a barroom at the forward end and a ladies' parlor at the stern. The American game of brag, now known as poker, was a common diversion, and gamblers used brag and three-card monte to fill their pockets.

The museum built a 30-foot model of a typical upper Mississippi River steamboat, "the largest model in captivity." The exterior walls of the one-eighth-scale model have been cut away to show the pilot, a rich banker, a barber, and even a peeping tom, each five inches tall.

"When I was a boy, there was but one permanent ambition among me and my comrades on the west bank of the Mississippi, and that was to be a steamboat man." That was the dream of young Sam Clemens, who fulfilled his destiny by becoming a Mississippi River pilot and, later, one of America's most colorful writers, Mark Twain. On the steamboat, Twain found mobility, elegance, and the door to opportunity. He also found disaster when the explosion of the packet boat *Pennsylvania* killed his brother Henry.

Getting upstream for a big race caused a few explosions, but not as many as were caused by a sleeping or absent engineer when the boats were in port. And snags disabled

194
Model of steam-powered towboat
Sprague *in boatyard diorama*

195
Woodward Riverboat Museum and the
Black*'s 25¹/₂-foot paddlewheel*

195

more steamboats than explosions, fires, and collisions combined. The average life of a steamboat was five years, and dangers aboard the steamboats were publicized by their chief competitor, the railroad, which published *Lloyd's Steamboat Directory and Disasters on the Western Waters* in 1856.

In the museum, a seven-foot pilot's wheel from the steamer *Arcola* stands among engine room telegraphs, running lights, nameboards, speaking tubes, and a steamboat pilot house from the towboat *Aquila*. River author Richard Bissel and his brother Fred offered the owner of the *Aquila* fifty dollars for whatever they could take off the sunken steamboat in the 1950s. The deal made, they cut the pilot house off the boat, turned it upside down, and floated it downriver to a point where they could lift it out. For some twenty years it served as a backyard playhouse, until it was given to the museum and restored.

From the 1830s to 1915, the upper Mississippi was the shipping artery for the logging states of Wisconsin and Minnesota, and great rafts of white pine were floated to downriver mills. At first they came down with the current, steered by men on sweeps or giant oars. By the 1860s, however, the steamboat was used to push the wooden rafts. Eventually, another steamboat was put at the front as a bowboat to steer the huge rafts, which often extended for acres. The value of lumber brought down the Mississippi in this fashion is estimated in the billions of dollars. Along with its collection of a logging brand axe, log chains, and other artifacts, the museum has built a ten-foot-square section of log raft, each log mounted on springs. Visitors "float" on the log raft, which appears to be four times its size because of full-length mirrors on two sides.

For over a century, Dubuque was a boatbuilding center, constructing vessels for the Mississippi River packet companies, the lumber trade, the Corps of Engineers, the Coast Guard, the Navy, and private boat owners, including the king of Siam. Beginning in 1870, the Iowa Iron Works built the *Clyde*, the first iron-hulled boat built for commercial use on the Mississippi River. Experiments with different forms of paddlewheel propulsion followed, including a contraption called the Dowler wheel, which soon became known as "Dowler's Humbug."

By the 1890s, the Iowa Iron Works began pursuing bigger business and landed a contract to build the torpedo boat *Ericsson* for the U.S. Navy. Launched in 1894, the *Ericsson* was capable of steaming at 25 knots. Over the objections of her Dubuque builders, the boat's pistons were built too light. When they broke during her trials in 1896, the Navy levied a penalty, which temporarily forced the company out of business. Influential U.S. Senator William B. Allison, a resident of Dubuque, protested and attached an amendment to a Navy appropriations bill, threatening to close the Navy down if they insisted on closing down the bankrupt Iowa Iron Works.

In 1901, the Iowa Iron Works built the *Sprague*, the world's largest steam-powered towboat. Construction of the 318-foot *Sprague* with her forty-by-forty-foot paddlewheel reportedly took three trainloads of steel, including two full carloads of rivets.

At one time, railroads had navies, sidewheel transfer boats used to ferry trains across the lower Mississippi. The boatyard now named the Dubuque Boat and Boiler Works built several. The boatyard built the *Orleander*, a U.S. Government boat that President Taft used on an inspection tour of the Mississippi. According to tradition, the corpulent Taft, weighing in at over 300 pounds, got himself stuck in the *Orleander*'s bathtub and required an application of grease before he was released.

In the 1920s and '30s, the Dubuque Boat and Boiler Works built several boats for the Federal Barge Line, a government attempt to revitalize river shipping. A volunteer at the museum who worked for the Federal Barge Line boats during this period recalls being ordered to fill the downriver barges with water to make them appear full, the low-floating barges thus assuring the farmers along the riverbank that the federal initiative was working.

In 1931, the boatyard built the *Herbert Hoover*, the world's largest diesel towboat of that era, and during World War II the yard was an important design facility for the Navy. Reflecting the affluence and leisuretime opportunities of post–World War II Americans, the company became a leader in excursion-boatbuilding in the 1950s and 1960s before it closed in 1972.

A 170-square-foot diorama shows the boatyard at the turn of the century when it was the largest boatyard on the inland waters. The collections include riveting guns, hog chains, a doctor pump (boiler feed pump which cured the steamboats of what ailed them—explosions), and a beer bucket used by the men to get a nickel's worth of beer during break. The museum archives contain extensive holdings of company blueprints, financial records, and correspondence.

Families as well as working men used the river, enjoying its recreational potential in vessels such as a now-restored 1905 double-ended gas-powered pleasure boat. When given to the museum, the boat was lodged in a grove of trees with a twelve-foot maple growing out of its center—nothing that a chain saw couldn't take care of. However, the hull of the boat was so fragile it had to be supported with a netlike crisscross of rope and lifted out of the woods by volunteers from a local college fraternity.

Easterners would be in for a big surprise if they believed a Mississippi River clam was a culinary treat. The meat of the Mississippi clam was fed to hogs or used as catfish bait; the real treasure was the shell, which was used to make pearl buttons, and an occasional pearl. The shell game was played from 1891, when John F. Boepple of Muscatine, Iowa, opened the world's first fresh water pearl button manufacturing plant until the late 1940s, when plastic crowded pearl buttons off the market.

The path from river bottom to shirtfront started with a clammer in a john boat who

196

used pairs of crowfoot bars to rake a clam bed on the river bottom. The clams closed on the hooks, catching themselves. The clammer pulled one crowfoot from the water, hundreds of clams attached, and dropped the other bar in. This process was then repeated over and over again.

On shore, the clams were "boiled out" and the meat separated from the shell. Shells were purchased by button companies who plied up and down the river in barges. High-speed drills cut several button blanks from each shell. The blanks were then polished, drilled for buttonholes, and carded. The museum depicts this era with a life-size clamming scene complete with john boat, crowfoot bars, shells, and buttons.

In addition to clamming, three thousand commercial fishermen were active on the upper Mississippi at the turn of the century. Fishing nets and catfish traps in the collections attest to the popularity of this industry. Small boats in the collections include a fishing flatboat, a clamming john boat, and two runabouts. The museum also exhibits a skiff,

196
Detail of a cut-away steamboat model

called a "quincy," used in log rafting, a logging bateau, a racing shell, canoes, a 32-foot houseboat, and a 43-foot diesel towboat.

The huge sidewheel steamboat *William M. Black* is probably the most impressive, and certainly the largest, of the museum's many fine acquisitions. It is one of the last of the steam-powered riverboats. Built in 1934 for the U.S. Army Corps of Engineers, the 277-foot *Black* was used to open and maintain the navigable channels of the Missouri and Mississippi rivers. The *Black* dredged the river bottom at a rate of 80,000 cubic yards a day, consuming 4,000 to 7,000 gallons of oil per day, with a minimum crew of 49 men. The boat was decommissioned in 1973.

Capable of housing 69 crew members, the steamboat *Black* was a home away from home for the men, as tours of duty could last up to two months. The main deck contains the engines, pumps, and other equipment necessary to propel the boat and dredge the river bottom. The second deck provided staterooms, a crew bunkroom, a galley, mess

197
Detail of a cut-away steamboat model showing ladies' cabin

halls for the officers and crew, and separate recreation rooms for officers and crew. A laundry for washing clothes was next to the dry room, with its clothesline hung over the vents above the boilers. The dollar hole was a trash chute just forward of the port paddlewheel, where the cook threw the unusable leftovers. When the garbage hit the water the paddlewheel churned it up and the waste was left behind.

In the machine shop an ice-cream maker was hooked up to a lathe and a recipe for "Dredge Black" homemade ice cream was discovered in the files. Every Friday, the crew had a fish fry on the stern of the *Black*, cooking the fish on the blacksmith's forge. The museum has re-created this event, serving fish from the forge, and tapes have played 1930s radio music and steamboat engine sound effects, while costumed figures take positions aboard the *Black*.

At the time the *Black* was acquired, a huge challenge was posed. The vessel is 85 feet wide; a floodwall protecting the city of Dubuque and the Ice Harbor is 73½ feet wide. After towing the boat from Gasconade, Mississippi, the museum had to get it into the harbor. In order to do this, 15 feet on one side of the *Black* had to be cut off, mainly deck overhang, but also the paddlewheel housing and the thirty-two-ton paddlewheel itself. With just 14 inches to spare on either side, the trimmed-down *William M. Black* squeezed through the floodwall gates. The paddlewheel housing was reassembled, floored over, and turned into a paddlewheel theater. The 25½-foot-diameter paddlewheel now stands in front of the museum, symbolic of the steamboat age.

In 1977, a vision of a museum of the Upper Mississippi River was shared by only a few. For the Dubuque County Historical Society, with one employee and an annual budget of $13,000, creation of the Woodward Riverboat Museum was an awesome undertaking.

Three giant strokes of the paddle started the museum moving: a $200,000 challenge pledge from the Dubuque-based Woodward Foundation, a gift of a waterfront freighthouse on the Mississippi, and a matching grant from the Maritime Department of the National Trust for Historic Preservation, its largest on the inland waters. A Mississippi River quest had begun, a quest for artifacts, for exhibit concepts, and for the financial means to build the museum.

The first artifact was the gift of the *William M. Black*. The football-field-size paddlewheeler became the museum's first and largest exhibit, almost a museum within itself. Then came more artifacts, a steamboat pilot house, and fishing, clamming, and logging boats. A research grant from the National Endowment for the Humanities as well as funding from private and corporate sources and all levels of government—federal, state, county, and city—followed. Now, some ten years and $2 million later, the museum employs thirty people and has a budget exceeding a half million dollars annually. Besides the vast sidewheel steamboat, which is moored at the Dubuque Ice Harbor, the museum

198
Aerial view of the side-wheeler William M. Black *and the* Woodward Riverboat Museum

199
Costumed figure of engineer in the Black*'s engine room*

198

199

WOODWARD RIVERBOAT MUSEUM 211

has a 10,000-square-foot exhibition gallery, a diesel towboat, thirteen smaller boats, two early-twentieth-century boathouses, and a new museum underway—the National Rivers Hall of Fame.

200
Double-ended pleasure boat, ca. 1905

This newest project is an impressive facility adjacent to the Woodward Museum. It tells the story of the men and women of all the inland waters of the United States, from pilots to poets, from engineers to inventors—the people who have had a significant impact on the waters of America.

Collections include six boats and sixteen boat models, boatbuilding tools, and an 8-foot model of the snagboat *Horatio G. Wright*, built for the St. Louis World's Fair and Exposition in 1904.

The Hall of Fame has also acquired a hammered copper steamboat eagle, circa 1891, that once perched atop the pilot houses of several steamboats, including the pleasure boats of the Mayo brothers of Mayo Clinic fame and, later, the U.S. Army Corps of Engineers boat *General Allen*. A bullet hole under the right wing of the eagle attests to an unexpected danger of Mississippi riverboat piloting, being fired upon by a sniper who took a pot shot at the eagle from a bluff top along the river.

The National Rivers Hall of Fame maintains an archive of river-related materials and is the national repository for the Mississippi River Parkways Commission and the Great River Road Association. It works closely with the National Park Service and the Maritime Department of the National Trust for Historic Preservation in the inventory and evaluation of maritime resources throughout the country.

From the dugout canoe to the sidewheeler *William Black*, from the keelboat cannon to the clamming crowfoot, the collections of the Woodward Riverboat Museum document a fascinating maritime epoch. The museum tells of the Indian rivermen, fierce battles for the lead mines, development of the Mississippi steamboat, and the building of the world's largest steam-powered towboat, the *Sprague*, in 1901.

These momentous developments, as well as the everyday works of fishermen and clammers, are enthusiastically recorded and documented at the Woodward Riverboat Museum. The exhibitions define the rich heritage of a mighty river—the Mississippi—and its awe-inspiring passage through five states and three hundred years. The museum's newest offspring, the National Rivers Hall of Fame, expands the focus to all of America's rivers and to the men and women who sought their destiny upon them.

200

THE GALVESTON HISTORICAL FOUNDATION

12 *'Elissa's' Return to Historic Galveston*
Peter H. Brink, Executive Director

The Galveston Historical Foundation

GALVESTON · TEXAS

On December 26, 1883, the three-masted barque *Elissa*, flying the Red Duster of Great Britain, measuring 202 feet from tip to tip, and manned by a crew of thirteen, slipped into the bustling Port of Galveston. Drawing only fourteen feet when loaded, she had passed safely over the sandbars at the harbor's entry, thus avoiding the slow process of lightering necessary for deeper draft ships. With her sails already doused, *Elissa* relied on a steam tugboat to nudge her alongside Labadie Wharf, one of numerous wooden piers jutting from the Strand to the channel's edge.

Elissa's arrival was scarcely noticed. She unloaded her cargo of bananas from Tampico, and in a few days would depart with a load of cotton for Liverpool, continuing to carry her assorted cargoes on routes around the world, whenever and wherever work was to be had.

Elissa was a graceful ship. She was built in 1877 in Aberdeen at the distinguished shipyard of Alexander Hall & Co., was owned by Henry Fowler Watt of Liverpool, and was named after the owner's niece. But even with her iron hull, *Elissa* was in many ways past her time. By the 1870s maritime commerce was turning more and more to larger vessels and to steam power. Watt's building of *Elissa* seems to have been motivated as much by his love of finely designed sailing ships as by the hard economics of her prospects.

Everywhere around *Elissa* on this day in Galveston were the clamor and frenzied activity of Texas' largest port. The big fleet of "red" Morgan ships, the Mallory steamers, and a variety of sailing vessels carried out cotton to Le Havre, Bremen, and Liverpool, as well as to American ports on the East Coast. Imports included an array of manufactured and household goods, as well as lumber, quarried stone, and other building materials, the latter items serving a dual role as ballast on the numerous ships inbound to load cotton. Sturdy immigrants arrived from Germany, Ireland, Scotland, Italy, Greece, and elsewhere to settle in Galveston or fan out to new communities across the Southwest. Mixed in with these oceangoing vessels were scores of riverboats and small craft, bringing in fresh produce, oysters, shrimp, and other local items in a lively bay and coastal trade.

201
Preceding pages: Elissa *salutes the Statue of Liberty, July 2, 1986, prior to centennial celebration*

202
Crew members aloft, furling royal and t'gallant sails on mainmast.

203

Part and parcel of this shipping activity, and abutting the wharves, were the hundreds of Victorian commercial buildings in The Strand area, housing everything from shipping agents, cotton factors, and insurance firms, to banks, commission houses, and wholesale emporiums, with a sprinkling of saloons and hotels. In total these formed the financial and commercial center of Texas and nearby states, so that the Strand, originally named after the street in London, was soon dubbed "The Wall Street of the Southwest."

All in all, some 95 percent of the merchandise brought by sea into Texas passed through the Port of Galveston. Indeed, the port's dominance was so great that some called her "the octopus of the Gulf." And the *Galveston Daily News* could taunt her upstart neighbor Houston for her inaccessibility to oceangoing ships; when barges of salt owned by Galveston merchant Samson Heidenheimer tipped over in Houston's bayou, the headline blared: HOUSTON BECOMES SALT-WATER PORT. GOD PROVIDES THE WATER AND HEIDENHEIMER THE SALT.

Yet, for all of Galveston's success in the latter 1800s, hers was a precarious location for a major city, perched as she was on the end of a barrier island a few feet above sea level.

203
Elissa *in dry dock in Piraeus, Greece, for replacement of rusted iron hull plates: the beginning of restoration*

204

Though visited by Indians, Spanish explorers, and occupied for a time by pirate Jean Lafitte, the permanent city was only established when entrepreneurs bought the island from the Republic of Texas in 1839. Its natural harbor attracted investors and settlers to this land of opportunity, eager to build a city destined, they were sure, to be "the Manhattan of the West."

On September 8, 1900, Galveston's vulnerability was laid bare when a massive hurricane devastated the city. In all, 6,000 persons were killed in the worst natural disaster of our nation's history.

Galveston responded with two magnificent feats. First, a massive seawall was built. Second, in an engineering miracle, the grade level of most of the city was raised an average of five feet.

Yet Galveston's attempted return to power as the dominant port in Texas was not to be. In 1914 Houston completed the Houston Ship Channel, linking her railroad hub directly to ocean commerce. The Port of Galveston, and thus the entire city, began a slow economic stagnation.

204
Elissa *in strong winds during 1986 day sails*

The hidden blessing of Galveston's boom-and-bust cycle was that a great majority of her Victorian structures were not demolished. By the late 1960s Galvestonians began realizing they had a collection of nineteenth-century architecture rarely equalled in the country. By 1973 a concerted effort to preserve and restore the Strand was underway, spearheaded by the Galveston Historical Foundation (GHF), a community-wide nonprofit historic preservation organization.

It was at this point, through coincidence and luck, that the paths of the barque *Elissa* and this star-struck city crossed once again.

By the 1970s *Elissa*, frail and rusting, was awaiting the salvage yards in Piraeus, Greece. Sold by Watt in 1897, she had sailed under the Norwegian flag as *Fjeld*, and then under the Swedish flag as *Gustav*. Subsequent owners had converted her to a motor ship, reduced her rig to a single cargo mast amidship, and even snubbed her distinctive Aberdeen clipper bow. Most recently, flying the Greek flag as *Christophoros* and hardly distinguishable from other small Mediterranean motor ships, she had been used to smuggle cigarettes from Yugoslavia to Italy.

Yet, despite all this, the keen eye of marine archaeologist Peter Throckmorton had perceived the lines of a nineteenth-century sailing vessel in this much-altered ship, and his subsequent investigation yielded the builder's plaque in place: Alexander Hall & Co. Upon learning this, Karl Kortum and the San Francisco Maritime Museum purchased *Elissa* to save her from the scrapyard, and for five years they hunted gallantly for a purchaser willing and able to undertake her preservation and restoration.

Nearly half a world away, Michael Creamer of the South Street Seaport Museum was visiting Galveston and, by chance, met local preservationist Paul Gaido, who, on learning of Michael's work, declared that The Strand's restoration would never be complete without a ship. And so it began. Within weeks Creamer, the romantic ship model builder, and Gaido, the passionate restaurateur, as if inspired by some divine force, had learned of *Elissa*, inspected her, and convinced GHF to obtain an option on her.

Thank heaven for dreams and blissful ignorance! With visions of a restored *Elissa*, masts towering, white sails billowing, bow cutting across the Atlantic bound for Galveston, a project was launched that was ultimately to take 8 years and $4 million . . . and to be one of the finest maritime restorations in the world.

To raise initial funds, the newly formed *Elissa* Committee sold cotton candy at festivals, held maritime auctions, and appealed for donations. By 1974 GHF had accumulated the $40,000 needed to purchase *Elissa*, and in 1976 a team of volunteers under the direction of Michael Creamer and Walter Rybka, also from South Street Seaport, left for Greece to begin restoration—an effort soon dubbed "the Greek Campaign." Much was accomplished: the hold cleared of cement, 25 percent of the hull plating replaced, and the Aberdeen bow restored. Yet, even as *Elissa* slid from the drydock with the blessing of a

205
Elissa *with sculptured figurehead and ornate trail boards, at berth in Galveston*

205

Greek Orthodox priest, it was painfully clear that the cost and complexity of the project precluded completion in Greece. In 1978–79, with towing charges skyrocketing at the height of the oil embargo, a last-gasp effort succeeded in bringing *Elissa*, on her own bottom if not under her own power, to Galveston . . . in the fervent hope that the ship's presence there would breathe new life into work on the Herculean task ahead.

What an arrival! Despite a coat of whitewash, *Elissa*'s beauty lay almost entirely in the eyes of those who already loved her. A hull with rotten decks, no masts, no sails, and not a speck of bright work left too much to the imagination for most people. Walter Rybka likened it to the "emperor's new clothes": *We* kept describing *Elissa* as a triumph, but inevitably people whispered, far and wide, that it was really an ugly hulk, far from the Tall Ship promised.

Existing funds were exhausted and debt incurred. Yet, in an unprecedented action, *Elissa* had been listed on the National Register of Historic Places while still in Greece, and GHF had recently gained approval of a $500,000 Federal challenge grant. At this point David Brink, yet another South Street Seaport veteran (and the writer's brother), was asked to evaluate GHF's options. He recommended closing the project down, as being beyond our resources. The *Elissa* Committee and GHF Board held fast and voted to persevere. David Brink and Walter Rybka then narrowed the project with board approval: the goal would continue to be a first-rate museum ship, fully operational, but sailing would be more limited than the extensive sea experience once envisioned. David was hired as *Elissa* Director, and a do-or-die two-year effort was launched to complete restoration.

Renewed fundraising efforts were met with generosity by a wide range of donors, so that funds stayed ahead—barely—of the feverish pitch of restoration work. With initial funds in hand, the hundreds of skilled processes essential to re-creating an 1877 ship moved forward with a passion under Walter's technical direction. He and other experts researched Alexander Hall ships (nearly all of *Elissa*'s original plans having been destroyed in a World War II air raid) and produced a stream of drawings to guide the work. Once our labor crew (the "Bilge Rats") had cleared away rotten decks and debris, skilled craftsmen renewed steel beams and hatches, riveted bulwarks and hull fittings, formed magnificent Oregon trees into masts and yards, and laid the deck of Douglas fir, caulked with oakum and pitch. Craftsmen parceled and served the standing rigging, reproduced the original teak rails and period woodwork, fabricated the multitude of sails, then stepped the masts, rigged all of this, and, finally, after nearly two years of work, fitted in place the sculpted figurehead, repainted the hull, and secured the interpretive panels. A labor of love had been completed. A Tall Ship had arisen, ghostlike, over the low wharves of Galveston.

On July 4, 1982, *Elissa*, once again a gleaming iron barque, was opened to the public at her permanent berth adjacent to The Strand. *Elissa* once again graced the Port of

206
Crew members attach running rigging, preparing to "bend on" upper topsail.

Galveston. This time, however, she was noticed, and loved. With hundreds cheering she was officially rechristened *Elissa* by Galveston grande dame Mary Moody Northen and dedicated as a maritime museum.

By the next day, even as *Elissa* began her new life as a museum ship, her volunteers were beginning sail training. For *Elissa* both looks as she did in 1877 and, in fact, is operational as she was then. Thus, in September of 1982, under the command of Captain Carl Bowman, *Elissa* slipped out of Galveston Harbor in all her glory, sailed the Gulf of Mexico, and brought to crew members and guests alike a sense of the grace and strength that had enabled her to crisscross the oceans of the world.

Elissa is a living ship. She sails, and she is cared for through the devoted work of staff and an amazing array of volunteers. Teachers, doctors, Johnson Space Center staff, students, artists, geologists, lawyers, entrepreneurs, retired persons, and manual workers are drawn together by the common bond of *Elissa*. As one volunteer states:

> I wanted to be a part of the restoration of *Elissa* because it is our past and future history. I'm not a "craftsman of the sea," but I knew *Elissa* needed free help. I could carry supplies, hold the end of a board; I knew I could do the "grunt work" and love every minute.

Out of this love, volunteers work with staff almost every weekend to help maintain the ship: stripping and revarnishing the teak, washing down the decks, tarring the standing rigging, replacing manila lines, and a myriad of other tasks, as well as delighting visitors with their tales of the ship.

By this work, volunteers gain the opportunity to become part of *Elissa*'s sailing crew. Each year fifty to seventy volunteers gather to undergo a rigorous course of sail training: learning the 162 lines and pin-rail diagram, knots and line handling, sequences and commands for raising and lowering sail, coming about, and, especially, working aloft. To a landlubber the experience of climbing up the shrouds, over the top and crosstrees, and then out on the yards, delicately balanced on the foot rope and at least one hand tightly gripping the jackstay, is both terrifying and exhilarating. Only with the caring support of experienced volunteer crew members do beginners overcome the initial fear and, step by step, repetition by repetition, learn to work aloft with a sureness, composure, and pride that would have seemed out of reach on the first venture up. Slowly the newcomer enters the family of the crew.

It is this dedication, joined with the technical expertise of Walter Rybka, the vision of David Brink, and the support by the Galveston Historical Foundation and generous donors, that has allowed the *Elissa* project to flourish. From this came *Elissa*'s crowning achievement to date: the voyage to New York to take her place as the oldest of the Class A vessels in the Parade of Tall Ships celebrating the Statue of Liberty Centennial on July 4, 1986.

207
Crew members work the capstan to adjust docking lines.

208
Crew members haul on main brace.

209
Heavy seas and brisk winds during an autumn 1986 day sail

207

208

209

It was on a sunny Memorial Day that *Elissa*, buoyed by a spirited Galveston send-off, began her long voyage to New York under the command of Captain Jay Bolton. A Tall Ship, yes . . . but she seemed so small, even frail, as one contemplated the 2,000-mile voyage ahead. One could not help but think of the recent tragedy of the *Pride of Baltimore* only days before, in the very waters *Elissa* would be crossing—for the *Pride*, a reproduction of a nineteenth-century Baltimore clipper, had been struck by a violent squall on May 14 while sailing north of Puerto Rico, and had sunk in less than 60 seconds. The captain and three of the twelve crew members had been lost. Our hearts had gone out to the crew and families of the *Pride*, and now *Elissa*, full of our friends and family, was embarking on a similar voyage.

Elissa's departure was a miracle in itself. The fervent dream of David Brink had enabled all obstacles to be overcome. The New York project had slipped through a window of opportunity before falling oil prices severely constricted the Texas economy. And an anonymous American visionary from Houston had responded beyond all limits of reasonableness when David and the writer had made our crucial requests. In all, more than $800,000 was given by hundreds of donors to refit *Elissa* with an engine room and auxiliary power and to carry out the Trip to Liberty . . . and this done while GHF was simultaneously completing a $4 million capital campaign.

Elissa's voyage, with stops at six ports en route, was maritime preservation at its finest. Day sails out of Charleston and Annapolis enabled land and ship preservationists to experience together this historic ship sailing as it was meant to sail. Guests joined in with gusto to haul on the lines and to venture up the shrouds for a taste of being aloft. In Baltimore, *Elissa* solemnly appeared at memorial services in the Inner Harbor to pay tribute to the *Pride* and lost members of her crew. In Washington, members of Congress and other leaders shared the ship and, throughout the voyage, special receptions and exhibits by the National Trust for Historic Preservation and the National Maritime Historical Society introduced thousands to maritime preservation.

On board *Elissa*, thirty volunteer crew members (over one hundred were rotated during the course of the trip) were each serving two four-hour watches each day and then working long hours to make *Elissa* sparkle for the parade in New York. Makeshift cots had been secured in the hold as sleeping quarters, with this eerie dormitory quickly dubbed "Camp *Elissa*." The few reporters and guests on board quickly found themselves commandeered as part of the crew, serving watches, doing cleanup, stripping varnish, and learning the ropes. (One reporter asked, "Was *Elissa* ever a slave ship?" and was told by a tired volunteer, "Not until GHF owned her.")

On June 30, *Elissa* set sail from Norfolk on the final leg to New York, now accompanied by three larger Tall Ships. *Elissa*'s volunteer crew felt a surge of pride as she became part of this breathtaking flotilla.

210
Crew members loose sails on foremast and mainmast.

211
Working aloft while the ship is underway requires caution and skill.

210

211

On the rainy morning of July 2, *Elissa* slipped into a New York Harbor enveloped by fog and mist. Crew members stared mesmerized as finally the tops of Manhattan's skyscrapers slowly and silently appeared, suspended in the grayness. *Elissa*, alone, glided past, and reached the Statue of Liberty. In the soft, misty quiet, crew members felt the moment complete: "We've done it . . . *Elissa* has reached New York. This is *our* time . . . tomorrow, we will share her with the world."

On July 4, sun shining and sparkling waves slapping her sides, *Elissa* boarded some ninety guests who had helped bring her to New York and took her place in the parade line-up off Sandy Hook. *Elissa* stopped once as Captain Bolton gladly agreed to take on board some ten French, Mexican, and U.S. guests who had missed their own ships and were stranded, a fitting coincidence as we paid tribute to Liberty with her flame of welcome. Then, *Elissa*, sails billowing, United States and Texas flags flying, slowly made her way up a Hudson River tumultuous with thousands of smaller boats, millions of spectators lining the shores, the carrier *John F. Kennedy*, and the presidential reviewing stand. With hearts full, we cheered and cheered and cheered the Statue of Liberty.

That evening, *Elissa* returned to a berth at South Street Seaport Museum, where being on the deck of *Elissa* was like being on stage, surrounded by tens of thousands of visitors crowding the piers and elevated platforms. With darkness the magnificent fireworks display lighted up the sky in dazzling colors to honor the Statue—and, at the same time, to celebrate, or so it seemed, *Elissa* and her gallant voyage.

On August 2, *Elissa* returned to Galveston safe and sound, scarred only by a broken jibboom from a squall off Bermuda. To the cheers of some 20,000 friends, *Elissa* glided into Galveston harbor and took her place of honor once again at the historic waterfront.

And so, through the dreams, hard work, and courage of many, this survivor from the Age of Sail lives in historic Galveston.

Snatched from the jaws of the salvage yard, *Elissa* is now alive as a maritime museum and interpretive center, berthed just a few feet from where she docked on that chance call to Galveston more than a century ago. Her hundred-foot masts tower adjacent to The Strand, its Victorian structures carefully restored to their former grandeur and alive with the rush of commerce and people. *Elissa*, secure as a part of our maritime heritage and lovingly cared for, cruises the Gulf waters on regularly scheduled day sails and, as opportunities arise, sails forth to other ports both near and far.

Elissa exists as one of the special things in our world and, more, as a beacon to all who would venture forth in quests of the human spirit.

212
Autumn 1986: Elissa *motors into the Gulf of Mexico for day sails.*

212

The Rockport Apprenticeshop

ROCKPORT · MAINE

Governed by forces far to the east of us, the tide falls.

On the next tide but one—early tomorrow morning—our newly launched sixern *Waterwitch* will sail for a small island in the granite archipelago of Vinalhaven. Before that departure, certain ballasting tests, dependent upon a carefully conducted capsize drill, must take place in the creek just north of the 'Shop. When the tide runs out of this forty-six-degree body of water, that test is no longer possible.

The stern and superb masters—tide, weather, and the assured battering the angry sea will sooner or later deliver—are the imperatives. Certainly economics, pragmatism, ideals, and artistic creeds are components of the educational process of the Rockport Apprenticeshop. They should be and will remain. However, other components, imperatives far stronger than those devised by man, continue to govern the Apprenticeshop just as they have governed maritime history for millennia.

This is a hard and a fine bargain.

One of the primary architects of the Rockport Apprenticeshop is the rugged coast of Maine itself. It has always demanded much, or as Robert Peter Tristram Coffin, Maine biographer, writes about the people,

> "the sea has washed out
> all the softness in them."

Ours is not merely an effort to *interpret* our coast. It is an effort to meet the challenges that the ruggedness of tide, wind, weather, oak, and granite have always proffered and, some might say, imposed.

For us it is exactly those qualities, born of practice and process, *not* those born of interpretation, information, or nostalgia, that we most need as we close a decade of this century and open those of the next.

At the center of our efforts stands always a series of distinctive, traditional water-

213
Preceding pages: *The second in a series of three 38-foot 18th-century French-American gigs,* Egalité *sails by Indian Island Lighthouse off Rockport on a May afternoon.* Egalité *was built to establish the Atlantic Challenge, a contest of seamanship between Europe and North America*

214
Perseverance, *a Penobscot Bay pinky schooner, was built in 1984 from lines taken by Chapell & Lincoln Colcord and refined by Robert Baker*

216

215

craft under construction, the building of which involves the transfer of skills from an older generation to the next one through apprenticing. This active rather than static display is our major public exhibit. The Apprenticeshop was founded to sustain capability, for we have become a nation information-rich and experience-poor.

The perpetuation of marine skills is the primary need in the field of maritime preservation today, as it was in the hour of the Spanish Armada. We carry on the tradition of a combined use of hands, heart, and head—a continuity exemplified by folk artisans through the history of the land and the sea.

The visitor examines all of this from an open gallery and talks with one of our apprentices there, but what is seen and heard and smelled is far more than an exhibit. That smacks of a technical demonstration. The boats under construction and the half-eaten sandwich beside an 1870s Witherby paring chisel on the north workbench are equally valid components of the life of this institution. On reflection, it would be curatorially unthinkable to sweep away a sandwich that, in any case, is calculated to get someone

215
Laying out patterns for grown frame futtocks on line edge timber cut in Rockport for a Shetland Islands sixern

216
Preparing for lofting on the main floor of the Apprenticeshop

217

219

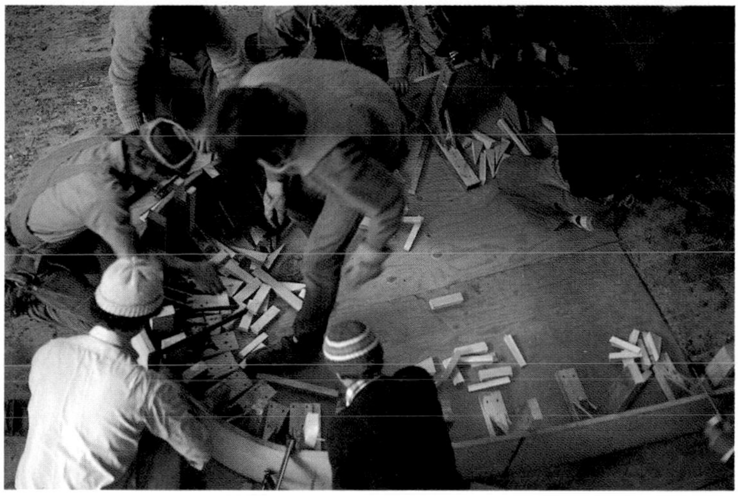

218

through the afternoon. Within this way of life, then, youth is the *agent*; the 'Shop is the *catalyst*. Plato spotted it all: "The one thing needful is training and testing."

Such a process demands the broadest interpretation of maritime history. Mine stems from a tutorial given me several decades ago by an older, wiry gentleman (journalists would have called him "grizzled") said to have been an Old China hand. Sitting on a crumbling seawall in the old port of Valetta, he illustrated his history by occasional reference to the cargo of a salt-, sweat-, and age-stained ditty bag with the name *HMS Basilisk*—later lost at Dunkirk, I believe—embroidered on it in heavily waxed sail twine.

His summary of all maritime history runs:

- Vintage wine aged in classic amphorae
- New wine into old bottles
- Broken bottles, plastic jugs
- Mutiny with purser dismembered; new wine in new amphorae

217
Apprentices work on the interior joinery of a Fenwick Williams 18-foot catboat, a classic design refined by Josef Liener

218
Half-hull modeling seminar. Students refer to a full-scale copy of subject model under construction in the 'Shop

219
Bending a $^7/_8$-inch coaming for a pinky schooner on a specially formed jig

220

221

I have not found a better. It fairly reeks of process, of *making*, and it is forged of exuberantly cyclical optimism. Most vital, it is truthfully, trenchantly redolent of the dollar, which must always be the true if unsung symbol of maritime history.

From Passamaquoddy on the Canadian border to the Piscataqua River and New Hampshire a scant one hundred years ago, communities formed around the imperatives of cutting granite, ice, or timber, rendering lime, and building shallops, barques, or schooners. In those communities men and women were artisans of necessity, making their own bread, medicine, and music. In Vinalhaven, Richmond, Camden, Clark and Hurricane islands, and Rockport they drew self-sufficiency from the land and sea. It was from the intensity of action and the immediate contact with raw materials and the elements that their strength of character, paradoxically the most abstract of their strengths, emerged. From the hewing axe and the star drill, from blizzards, tides, and dynamite, they attained tenacity, care, patience, humor, and wisdom that fashioned America and a hundred other nations and gave them the resilience to go on.

220
Fairing the caprail of a 24-foot Shetland Islands sixern

221
Finishing touches

222

223

224

Just as Melville selected his symbols from the denseness of reality (to a greater extent than any other writer whom I can bring to mind), so the most precious of abstract strengths proceed from the most tangible associations, the most experiential living. That transfer is the overriding, *lived* conviction here at the Apprenticeshop.

We've studied and copied those Maine coast communities and drawn what is applicable around again, the cyclical history of my friend of the seawall. An instance: we run a modified boardinghouse in a seven-building dwelling place on sixteen acres of land, largely designed and all constructed by our apprentices, staff, and volunteers. Those community precedents fascinate us. The grease on which they were always, always launched and run was skills. Our grease is . . . skills.

Gertrude Stein wrote: You can be modern, or
you can be a museum,
but you can't be both.

222
Cutting in the rabbet for a 32-foot double-ender, the Maine Quoddy Ketch

223
Plumbing the keel assembly for a 15-foot Washington County peapod

224
Instructor Vern Spinosa carves the billethead of the Robert H. Baker.

We must be. Therefore we are. We drive into the future looking constantly into the rearview mirror. The view there is not one of nostalgia—the diphtheria, the ice, the never-ending struggle, and the tantalizing distance from ease keep us from that. But that rearview mirror keeps us mindful of imperatives we will not surrender: Yankee ingenuity; making, not buying; recycling; celebrating in the heart of fatigue, strain, and paradox. For instance, the 'Shop trains through the hardest rather than the easiest boat-building method—plank on frame. We burden apprentices with demands which result in steady, stable competence just as the Grand Banks dory, when heavily burdened with cod, becomes more stable, more safe.

Such trials become a living metaphor at the 'Shop. Out the other side of dismantling a barn and scrounging apple knees, scrap lead, and firewood come a resilience and a kind of armor against the frequent helplessness or disheartenment of modern life.

Twenty years ago in an Outward Bound course, pulling across East Penobscot Bay in a pair of thirty-foot boats, two crews were caught by night and fog. We tethered those boats and rowed on, the initial crew complaining of the failure of the second boat to pull its weight. In the morning, standing on the Maine granite headland and looking out over that broad expanse of water, one of the students in the lead boat remarked, ''We're all tied together and you can't let go.'' And that is Ishmael tied irrevocably and wonderfully to Queequeg; that is the profound law of essential human bondage laid down by Melville 140 years ago—the same law learned straight from the Garden of Eden.

We have fashioned the Apprenticeshop in the image of a three-stranded rope, each part of which depends utterly on the others for its strength. No strand is more important than another. The first strand is an assertive philosophy that needs to be lived rather than professed. Just as those two boats were tethered together, so we learn at the Apprenticeshop both through and for the maritime skills of many nations. Kurt Hahn, the remarkable international educator and founder of Gordonstoun, Outward Bound, and Atlantic College, inspired the Rockport Apprenticeshop. He spoke of the ''decline of care and patience due to the weakened tradition of craftsmanship.'' We are not a vocational school, although some 70 percent of our graduates work in the field of maritime preservation from Mystic to San Diego, from Mount Desert to British Columbia, from the Maldive Islands to Brittany, from the National Maritime Museum in San Francisco to the *Elissa* project in Galveston. Our philosophy is a bold one of revitalizing functional art—learning for the trade and through the discipline of traditional boat-building. Thus landing the hood end of a northern cedar plank in the rabbet of a small lapstrake peapod is a defense, a ''benign attack'' on a culture which has become attuned primarily to flickering images, a culture which purchases rather than makes its artifacts.

In November 1985, we sailed our recently completed pinky schooner *Perseverance* and four other 'Shop boats down the coast to salvage a winter's firewood from the oak

225
Planing the stem of Liberté, *first one of the French-American gigs of the International Atlantic Challenge. The first Challenge took place in New York Harbor in front of the Statue of Liberty during the 1986 Operation Sail*

226

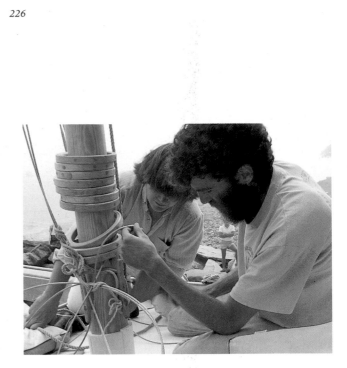

227

228

blowdowns of Hurricane Gloria. This spring, with the help of forty volunteers, we dismantled a major Camden building, the $9,000 worth of lumber to be recycled to extend the physical plant of the 'Shop and its living quarters. We have cut 150-year-old spar stock on an island in Englishman Bay and burnished the bronze gammon iron of a thirty-two-foot Quoddy Pilot. The second strand of the 'Shop, then, is fashioned of such gifts from the land and life around us.

The third strand is humanity. We pay more attention to people than to technology; the latter is used only to hone the former. Remember that north workbench? Even when the mayonnaise pours onto it from the starboard scuppers of that sandwich, the mess thereon becomes an integral part of the future of craftsmanship. Our brand of humanism

226
The pinky schooner Perseverance *making knots off Cape Ann, ''with a bone in her teeth''*

227
The pre-launch ''end game'' of the 20-foot sloop, Robert H. Baker

228
Learning rigging techniques

229   230

doesn't mean ease—we've built the living quarters and rebuilt much of the boatyard to sustain our process, to inform ourselves, and to inspire the public.

International exchange is as much a part of this community as sharpening the chisels or feeding Marsh, the 'Shop cat. There are overseas apprentices from Germany, Italy, and Scotland. We are publishing an English version of *Kågen*, a wonderful book on the construction of a Scandinavian fishing boat. It was translated by Annika Fallai, a Swede here with her family for six months during which her husband, Umberto, instructed us in Swedish boat-building. All of us learned of each other's cultures. Also being documented at the 'Shop is a series of Scottish craft built between 1882 and the 1930s. The resultant technical drawings will swell the archives of the Scottish Maritime

229
The sloop Robert H. Baker, *named after her designer*

230
Matinicus Island peapod, a long-standing favorite of the Apprenticeshop

Museum as well as our Technology Bank, which contains drawings, old and new photographs, taped discussions, and written material from sources as diverse as the South Pacific *proa* tradition, the prams of Norway, and the *feluccas* of both Italy and Tamales Bay, California.

One of the best dreams of maritime preservation is forging "scholar shipwrights" who will combine the cerebral skills with the manual. Thus, in addition to hands-on training for and through boat-building and seamanship, we are developing a Tech Bank through field research and documentation, and we publish prints, line drawings, and *The Apprentice*, the 'Shop's journal devoted to skills transfer, small craft, and international exchange.

Craftsmanship, particularly the building and handling of traditional small craft, is viewed and practiced here as "ambassadorial," linking the youth of nations in a "physical dialogue" to exchange information on construction and seamanship, recipes for chowder, songs, and rituals. One of the finest moves that an institution in our times can perform is to draw the youth of different countries into a conspiracy to provide continuity in the great practical arts of the sea and seaboard. Increasingly, we are consulting with individuals in other countries—most recently in France and in Scotland—who share this belief in the importance of instilling in young people a respect for the mastery of the sea and for the traditional ways in which this mastery has been achieved. We also recently consulted with American institutions, including the Galveston Historical Society, Plimoth Plantation, the National Maritime Museum, Cooper Union, the National Endowment for the Arts, and the Mayor's Youth Service Corps in New York, on programs that serve these values as well.

The conviction that young people both in this country and abroad are enriched through hands-on experience in the craft of seamanship stems from the following experience. Some years ago, walking through a superb maritime museum in an antique land, I fell to wondering about youth all around the Atlantic. In studying the work of their ancestors who fished Damariscove and the North Sea, rounded the Horn, and traded with China, Bali, or the inland sea of Japan, might they not look around and ask, with a validity as acute as it is sad, whether their culture and they themselves have not surrendered a primal relationship to the old, at once so-demanding and so-sustaining "physical world"? The way lies open to our feeling paltry in the face of such evidence.

And so we fashioned an apprentice program. At the center, we placed the traditional wooden boat, the reality and symbol of functional art, of youth training, and of demonstrable skills. Indeed, the Rockport Apprenticeshop was founded to provoke an *active*, not passive, response to the magnificence of our maritime patrimony.

Call it a new amphora.

231

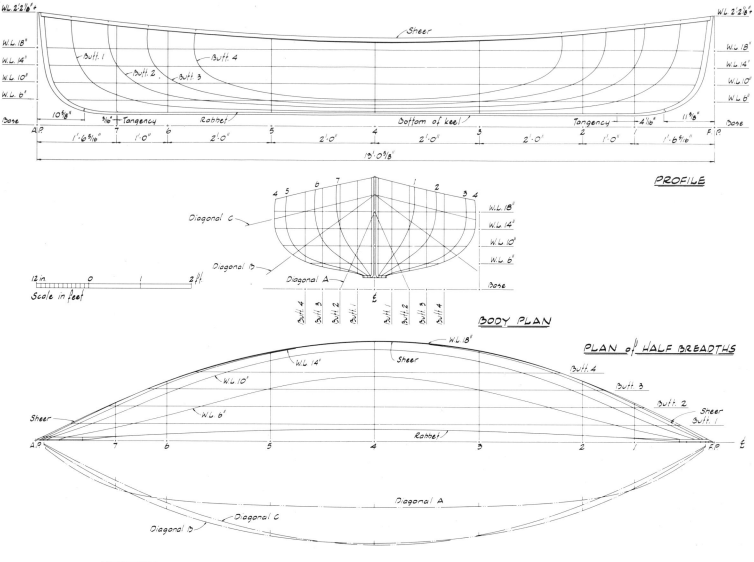

PROFILE

BODY PLAN

PLAN of HALF BREADTHS

Scale in feet

STERN OFFSETS from A.P.	Face	Rabbet
Sheer	0·0·2	0·1·4
W.L.18"	0·1·1	0·2·1
W.L.14"	0·1·5	0·2·6
W.L.10"	0·2·5	0·3·6
W.L.6"	0·5·3	0·7·0

STEM OFFSETS from F.P.		
Rabbet	Face	
0·1·4	0·0·2	Sheer
0·2·4	0·1·2	WL.18'
0·3·2	0·2·0	WL.14'
0·4·3	0·3·1	WL.10'
0·8·0	0·6·3	WL.6'

Lines to outside of carvel plank in
Feet·inches·eighths.
Perpendiculars taken at stem & stern rands.
Sheer is top of plank at side.
WL's & Butts spaced 4'
Diagonal A 18" up on ₵ 8" out on base
Diagonal B 22" up on ₵, 16" out on WL.10"
Diagonal C 22" up on ₵, 16" out on WL.18'
This boat was measured by the Apprentices.

TABLE of OFFSETS

		Stem	1	2	3	4	5	6	7	Stern
Heights above base	Sheer	2·2·0	1·11·7	1·10·5	1·9·2+	1·8·6+	1·9·3+	1·11·1	2·0·2	2·2·0
	Butt.4	·	·	·	0·7·6+	0·6·2+	0·7·5	·	·	·
	Butt.3	·	·	0·11·2	0·6·0	0·5·1	0·5·7+	0·11·3	·	·
	Butt.2	·	1·2·2	0·7·3+	0·4·6	0·4·2	0·4·7	0·7·2+	1·2·2+	·
	Butt.1	·	0·7·3	0·4·5+	0·3·6	0·3·4	0·3·6	0·4·5+	0·7·2	·
	Rabbet	·	0·3·1+	0·3·1	0·3·1	0·3·1	0·3·1	0·3·1	0·3·1+	·
	Keel	·	0·2·5+	0·2·5	0·2·5	0·2·5	0·2·5	0·2·5	0·2·5+	·
Half breadths from ₵	Sheer	·	0·9·1	1·2·1	1·8·7	1·10·7+	1·8·4	1·1·5	0·8·7	·
	WL.18"	·	0·8·6	1·9·0+	1·11·1	1·11·6+	1·8·3	0·8·6	·	·
	WL.14"	·	0·7·7+	1·1·3+	1·8·5	1·11·0	1·8·3	1·1·1	0·7·7	·
	W.L.10"	·	0·5·7	0·11·0	1·6·4+	1·9·1+	1·6·5	0·11·0	0·6·0+	·
	WL.6"	·	0·2·7	0·5·7	1·0·0	1·3·0	1·0·1+	0·5·7	0·3·0+	·
	Rabbet	0·0·6	0·1·0	0·1·4+	0·2·4	0·2·7	0·2·4	0·1·4+	0·1·0	0·0·6
	Diag.A	0·1·7	0·10·7	1·1·3+	1·2·7	1·3·2	1·2·7	1·1·4	0·11·1	0·1·7
	Diag.B	0·1·1	0·10·5	1·3·7	1·9·6+	1·11·4+	1·9·7	1·3·6	0·10·3+	0·1·1
	Diag.C	0·1·0	0·9·3	1·2·4	1·9·5	1·11·7	1·9·2	1·2·3	0·9·1+	0·1·0

232
Lines drawing, by draftsman David Dillion, of a North Haven peapod from the Technology Bank of the Rockport Apprenticeshop. A growing archive of technical drawings, photographs, and taped interviews concerning small craft, shipbuilding methods and tools, and nautical equipment comprise a critical element of the Apprenticeshop. Documentation of one-of-a-kind vessels, as well as the ways of handling them—indeed, of the intricate skills of self-sufficiency which their builders and users developed—is both a primary responsibility and a crucial function of maritime preservation.

List of Plates and Notes on Illustrations

De Jacob was commanded by Jan Kloorn of Den Helder for owner Jan Pos of Zaandam. The naive style of the painting is reminiscent of whaling scenes of similar vintage inscribed by and attributed to Johan Samuel Winkstern, in the collection of the Altonaer Museum, Hamburg.

34 "Bacchanalian Frolic," attributed to Jan Lutma the Elder and Jan Osborn, ca. 1618–41. Pressed baleen panel, 4 in. × 6¹/₂ in. (10.2 cm × 15.8 cm). The Kendall Whaling Museum (#S-1591). Photograph by Mark Sexton

35 "Ship *Hollandia* Whaling in Company on the Arctic Grounds," by Abram van Salm of Delftshaven, ca. 1702. Monochrome *penschildering* (pen-painting) or *grisaille* (gray painting) on panel, 26¹/₂ in. × 41³/₄ in. (67.3 cm × 106 cm). The Kendall Whaling Museum (#0-165). Photograph by Mark Sexton.

The technique originated in 17th-century Holland with Heerman Witmont, Ludolph Backhuyzen, and the Willem van de Veldes, who are its most celebrated practitioners.

36 "Greenland Whale Fishery," 18th century. Ensemble of 80 monochrome manganese faience tiles, 36¹/₂ in. × 47¹/₄ in. (92.7 cm × 120 cm). After the double-folio etching "Groenlandsche Visschery" (Greenland Whale Fishery) drawn by Sieuwert van der Meulen, etched by Adolph van der Laan, and published by Petrus Schenck, ca. 1720, 23¹/₂ in. × 39 in. (59.7 cm × 99 cm). The Kendall Whaling Museum (#0-250). Photograph by Mark Sexton.

Similar versions are known elsewhere, for example, in the collection of the Moraiaen Museum, Gouda.

37 "Japanese Whaling," by Kuniyoshi, ca. 1840. Woodblock print, 14¹/₂ in. × 30¹/₄ in. (36.8 cm × 76.8 cm). The Kendall Whaling Museum (#P-J3107-A). Photograph by Mark Sexton

38 "Whaling in the Polar Sea," by Ludolf Backhuyzen, ca. 1700. Oil on canvas, 38¹/₂ in. × 48¹/₂ in. (97.8 cm × 123.2 cm). Signed *Bakyz.* The Kendall Whaling Museum #0-126, photograph by Mark Sexton.

At about the same time of this painting, *De Vergulde Walvis* was commanded by Dirck Jandsz of Amsterdam.

39 "Whaleship *Frankendaal* of Amsterdam, Maarten Mooy of Callantsoog, Master, Whaling in Company on the Greenland Grounds, 1786," by Jan Mooy, 1843. Watercolor, 17¹/₈ in. × 24⁵/₈ in. (43.5 cm × 62.5 cm). The Kendall Whaling Museum (#0-5). Photograph by Mark Sexton.

The vessel *De Jager* was commanded by Jochum Blaauboer of St. Maartensbrug for the firm of Jongewaart & Tip of West Zaan, the *Groenlandia* by Dirk Cornelisz Duyn of De Rijp, for Klaas Tan & Son of Zaandam, and the *Frankendaal* by Maarten Mooy for Jan Gildmeester & Son, Amsterdam.

40 "British Whaling in the Arctic," by John Wilson Carmichael, 19th century. Oil on canvas, 42 in. × 63 in. (106.7 cm × 160 cm). The Kendall Whaling Museum (#0-350). Photograph by Mark Sexton

41 "Vae Victis—The *Cachalot* Cutting-In" by William Edward Norton, 19th century. Oil on canvas, 43¹/₂ in. × 59¹/₂ in. (110.5 cm × 151.1 cm). The Kendall Whaling Museum (#0-141). Photograph by Mark Sexton

One of a pair, the other of which is "The *Cachalot* Trying-Out at Night," based on the classic book by Frank T. Bullen, *Cruise of the Cachalot* (London and New York, 1898), the artist's copy of which the Kendall Whaling Museum also possesses.

42 Watercolor "Ship *Adam* of London Sperm-Whaling in the South Seas," anonymous, post-Napoleonic period. 11¹/₄ in. × 14¹/₄ in. (28.8 cm × 36.2 cm). Scrimshaw sperm-whale tooth, anonymous, post-Napoleonic period. 9¹/₄ in. (23.5 cm) long. The Kendall Whaling Museum (#0-398 and #S-1232). Photograph by Mark Sexton

43 "A Tough Old Bull," by William Heysman Overend (1851–98). Oil on canvas, 19³/₈ in. × 29 in. (49.2 cm × 73.7 cm). The Kendall Whaling Museum (#0-13). Photograph by Mark Sexton

44 American whaling memorabilia. The Kendall Whaling Museum (S/L/T). Photograph by Mark Sexton.

The whaling irons are a double-flue harpoon by Dean & Driggs, a toggle harpoon of a type invented ca. 1848 by black shipsmith Lewis Temple, made by J. & T. Durfee, and a lance by the Macy firm.

45 Shipboard paraphernalia of Frederick Howland Smith. Kendall Whaling Museum (#S-512 and S-513). Photograph by Mark Sexton.

The special canvas covers fashioned by Smith for his shipboard diaries had scraps and pockets for his whale-stamp, pipe, fid, and other personal articles. Smith took time out from his maritime career for a three-year stint as a foot soldier in the 18th Massachusetts Volunteers of the Union Army.

46 "A Norwegian Steam Whaler Striking his fish in the Varanger Fjord, July 1882, as witnessed from the deck of the S.S. Yacht *Pandora*," by George Earl, 1882. Oil on canvas, 34 in. × 49 in. (86.4 cm × 124.5 cm). The Kendall Whaling Museum (#0-411). Photograph by Schillay & Reys, Inc., New York, N.Y.

3 MYSTIC SEAPORT MUSEUM

47 Henry B. du Pont Preservation Shipyard. Mystic Seaport Museum. Photograph by Nancy d'Estang

48 Figurehead of *Seminole*. Mystic Seaport Museum. Photograph by Claire White-Petersen

49 *Telegram*, 1875. Mystic Seaport Museum. Photograph by E. A. Scholfield

50 "Sports of Whalemen," by Robert Weir, 1855–58. Mystic Seaport Museum. Photograph by Rodney Chalk

51 "*Neptune* on the Grand Bank of Newfoundland," by John E. C. Petersen, 1866. Mystic Seaport Museum. Photograph by Mary Anne Stets

52 "Clipper *Carlos C. Colgate*," by Jurgen Frederick Huge, 1869. Watercolor. Mystic Seaport Museum. Photograph by Mary Anne Stets

53 *Joseph Conrad.* Mystic Seaport Museum. Photograph by Claire White-Petersen

54 Sail-setting demonstration. Mystic Seaport Museum

55 *Sabino.* Mystic Seaport Museum. Photograph by Claire White-Petersen

56 Thomas Oyster Co. building. Mystic Seaport Museum

57 Winter scene. Mystic Seaport Museum. Photograph by Claire White-Petersen

58 Charles Mallory Sail Loft and the Plymouth Cordage Co. exhibit. Mystic Seaport Museum. Photograph by Mary Anne Stets

59 Captain's day cabin, *Benjamin F. Packard.* Mystic Seaport Museum. Photograph by Brad Smith

60 New York Yacht Club's original clubhouse. Mystic Seaport Museum. Photograph by Wick York

61 The James Driggs Shipsmith Shop. Mystic Seaport Museum. Photograph by Mary Anne Stets

62 Caulking the *Morgan.* Mystic Seaport Museum. Photograph by Mary Anne Stets

63 *Regina M.* Mystic Seaport Museum. Photograph by Claire White-Petersen

Appendix: Additional American Maritime Collections

Adirondack Museum
The Adirondack Historical Association
Blue Mountain Lake, NY 12812

Admiral Nimitz Center
P.O. Box 777
Fredericksburg, TX 78624

Allie Ryan Maritime
    Collection of Maine Museum
Box C-1
Maine Maritime Academy
Castine, ME 04420

American Merchant Marine Museum
U.S. Merchant Marine Academy
Kings Point, NY 11024

Antique and Classic Boat Society
P.O. Box 831
Lake George, NY 12845

Atlantic County Historical Society
P.O. Box 301
Somers Point, NJ 08244

Baltimore Seaport and Baltimore
    Maritime Museum
Pier Four, Pratt Street
Baltimore, MD 21202

Battleship *Texas* Historical Park
3527 Battleground Road
La Porte, TX 77571

Bay County Historical Society
1700 Center Avenue
Bay City, MI 48706

Bayfield Heritage Association Inc.
P.O. Box 137
Bayfield, WI 54814

Beaver Island Historical Society
St. James, MI 49782

Bellport-Brookhaven
    Historical Society and Museum
Seven Thornhedge Road
Bellport, NY 11713

Belvedere-Tiburon Landmarks Society
12 Beach Road
P.O. Box 134
Belvedere Tiburon, CA 94920

Beverly Historical Society and
    Museum
117 Cabot Street
Beverly, MA 01915

Boothbay Region Historical Society
P.O. Box 272
Boothbay Harbor, ME 04538

Border Historical Society
1 Capen Avenue
Eastport, ME 04631

Boston Tea Party Ship and Museum
Congress Street Bridge
Boston, MA 02129

Bostonian Society
Old State House
206 Washington Street
Boston, MA 02109

Brick Store Museum
Main Street
P.O. Box 177
Kennebunk, ME 04043

Buffalo Bill Museum of Le Claire,
    Iowa, Inc.
404 South Second Street
Le Claire, IA 52753

Buffalo Naval and Servicemen's Park
1 Naval Park Cove
Buffalo, NY 14202

C & O Canal of Cumberland, Md.,
    Inc.
300 Bel Air Drive
Cumberland, MD 21502

C.A.N.A.L., Inc.
36 Lakeview Avenue
Lincoln, RI 02865

Canal Museum, Hugh Moore Park
Box 877
Easton, PA 18042

Canal Park Marine Museum
U.S. Army Corps of Engineers
Duluth, MN 55802

Canastota Canal
Town Museum
122 Canal Street
Canastota, NY 13032

Cape Ann Historical Association
27 Pleasant Street
Gloucester, MA 09130

Cape Hatteras National Seashore
Route 1, Box 675
Manteo, NC 27945

Cape May Historical Museum
Route 9
Cape May Court House
Cape May, NJ 08210

Chesapeake Bay Maritime Museum
Navy Point
St. Michaels, MD 21663

Chicamacomico Historical Association
    Inc.
P.O. Box 140
Rodanthe, NC 27968

The Children's Museum
P.O. Box 3000
Indianapolis, IN 46219

Citadel Archives Museum
The Citadel
Charleston, SC 29409

City Island Historical Nautical
    Museum
190 Fordham Street
City Island
Bronx, NY 10464

Clatsop County Historical Society
441 Eighth Street
Astoria, OR 97103

Clausen Memorial Museum
P.O. Box 708
Petersburg, AK 99833

Clay County Historical Society
22 North Eighth
Moorhead, MN 56560

Coast Artillery Museum at Fort
    Worden
433 Ranger Drive, SE
Olympia, WA 98503

Coast Guard Museum of the North
    West
1519 Alaskan Way S
Seattle, WA 98134

Coastal Heritage Society
One Fort Jackson Road
Savannah, GA 31404

Cohasset Historical Society, Inc.
P.O. Box 324
Cohasset, MA 02025

Columbia River Maritime Museum
1792 Marine Drive
Astoria, OR 97103

Confederate Naval Museum
P.O. Box 1022
Columbus, GA 31902

Connecticut River Foundation at
    Steamboat Dock, Inc.
P.O. Box 261
Essex, CT 06426

Coquille River Museum
P.O. Box 737
390 SW First Street
Bandon, OR 97411

Corpus Christi Museum
1900 North Chaparrel
Corpus Christi, TX 78401

Cruiser *Olympia,* Submarine *Becuna*
    Association, Inc.
P.O. Box 928
Philadelphia, PA 91905

Custom House Maritime Museum
25 Water Street
Newburyport, MA 01950

Cairo Museum
P.O. Box 349
Vicksburg, MS 39180-0349

Deer Isle-Stonington Historical
    Society
Rural Free Delivery
Stonington, ME 04681

Del Norte County Historical Society
577 H Street
Crescent City, CA 95531

Door County Maritime Museum
6427 Green Bay Road
Sturgeon Bay, WI 54235

Dossin Great Lakes Museum
100 Strand/Belle Isle
Detroit, MI 48207

Dukes County Historical Society
Box 827
Edgartown, MA 02539

East Hampton Town Marine Museum
Bluff Road
Amagansett, NY 11930

Edmonds South Snohomish County
    Historical Society
P.O. Box 52
Edmonds, WA 98020

Erie Historical Museum
556 West Sixth Street
Erie, PA 16507

Fort Nisqually Museum
Point Defiance Park
Tacoma, WA 98407

Franklin Institute
20th and Benjamin
Franklin Parkway
Philadelphia, PA 19103

Friends of the *Jean*
3112 Seventh Street
Lewiston, ID 83501

Friends of *Nobska,* Inc.
128 Ocean Avenue
Cranston, RI 02905

Gloucester Fisherman's Museum
Rogers and Porter Street
Box 159
Gloucester, MA 01930

Grand Banks Schooner Museum Trust
11 Road's End
Boothbay Harbor, ME 04538

Great Lakes Maritime Institute
Belle Isle
Detroit, MI 48207

Great Lakes Historical Society
    Museum
480 Main Street
P.O. Box 435
Vermilion, OH 44089

Great Lakes Naval and Maritime
  Museum
P.O. Box A-3785
Chicago, IL 60690

Hampton Roads Naval Museum
Pennsylvania H. G-29
Norfolk Naval Base
Norfolk, VA 23511

Head of the Lakes Maritime Society
P.O. Box 775
Superior, WI 54880

Heritage Boat Club
2554 W. Pensacola Avenue
Chicago, IL 60610

Herreshoff Marine Museum
P.O. Box 450
18 Burnside Street
Bristol, RI 02809

Historical Society of Greater Port
  Jefferson
115 Prospect Street
Port Jefferson, NY 11777

Historical Society of Old Yarmouth
Two Strawberry Lane
Box 11
Yarmouth Port, MA 02675

Howard Steamboat Museum, Clark
  County Historical Society
1101 East Market Street
P.O. Box 606
Jeffersonville, IN 47130

Hull Lifesaving Museum
6 Circuit Avenue
Hull, MA 02045

Huron City Museum
7930 Huron City Road
Port Austin, MI 48467

Kentucky Library and Museum
Western Kentucky University
Bowling Green, KY 42101

Kittery Naval and Historical Museum
P.O. Box 453
Rogers Road
Kittery, ME 03904

Lahaina Restoration Foundation
Box 338
Lahaina, Maui HI 96767

Maine Maritime Museum
963 Washington Street
Bath, ME 04530

Manistee County Historical Museum
425 River Street
Manistee, MI 49660

Marblehead Historical Society
161 Washington Street
P.O. Box 1048
Marblehead, MA 01945

Marine Corps History and Museums
  Division
Building 58
Navy Yard
Washington, DC 20374

Mark Twain Home Board
208 Hill Street
Hannibal, MO 63401

Marquette County Historical Society
213 North Front St.
Marquette, MI 49855

Marquette Maritime Museum
1515 Lynn Street
Marquette, MI 49855

Maryland Historical Society
201 West Mount Street
Baltimore, MD 21201

Mason County Historical Society
1687 S. Lakeshore Drive
Ludington, MI 49431

Mattapoisett Historical Society
Main Street
Mattapoisett, MA 02739

Missouri Historical Society
Jefferson Memorial Building,
  Forest Pk.
St. Louis, MO 63112

Missouri River History Museum
P.O. Box 124
Brownville, NE 68321

Mohawk Corporation
901 Washington Street
Wilmington, DE 19801

Moosehead Marine Museum
P.O. Box 1151
Pritham Avenue
Greenville, ME 04441

Museo de Historia Militar y Naval de
  Puerto Rico
Fort Saint Jerome
P.O. Box 4184
San Juan, PR 00905

Museum of Arts and History
1115 Sixth Street
Port Huron, MI 48060

Museum of Coastal History
610 Beachview Drive
St. Simons Island, GA 31522

Museum of Fine Arts
465 Huntington Avenue
Boston, MA 02115

Museum of Florida History
R.A. Gray Building
Tallahassee, FL 32301

Museum of Natural History
Roger Williams Park
Providence, RI 02905

Museum of Science, Art and
  Industry, Inc.
4450 Park Avenue
Bridgeport, CT 06604

Museums of the City of Mobile
355 Government Street
Mobile, AL 36609

Mystic Seaport Museum, Inc.
Greenmanville Avenue
Mystic, CT 06355

MIT Museum, Hart Nautical
  Collections
265 Massachusetts Avenue
Cambridge, MA 02139

Muskogee War Memorial
Park Authority
P.O. Box 253
Muskogee, OK 74401

North American Wildfowl Art
  Museum of the Ward Foundation
Salisbury State College
Salisbury, MD 21801

Nantucket Historical Association
P.O. Box 1016
Nantucket, MA 02554

Nantucket Life Saving Museum, Inc.
Polpis Road
Nantucket, MA 02554

National Liberty Ship Memorial, Inc.
Fort Mason—Bldg 57
Washington Navy Yard
Washington, DC 20374

Naval UnderSea Warfare
  Museum Engineering Station
NUWES Code 05m
Keyport, WA 98345

Naval War College Museum
Coasters Harbor Island
Newport, RI 02841

Navy Memorial Museum
Washington Navy Yard
Building # 76
Washington, DC 20374

Navy Supply Corps Museum
Navy Supply Corps School
Athens, GA 30606

Navy, Marine Corps and Coast Guard
  Museum of the Pacific
Bldg 1, Treasure Island
San Francisco, CA 94130

Neversink Valley Area Museum, D
  and H Canal Park
D & H Canal Site
Box 263
Cuddebackville, NY 12729

New Bedford Whaling Museum
18 Johnny Cake Hill
New Bedford, MA 02740

New York State Historical Association
Lake Road
Box 800
Cooperstown, NY 13326

Noank Historical Society, Inc.
17 Latham Lane
Noank, CT 06340

North Carolina Marine Research
  Center, Fort Fisher
Fort Fisher
P.O. Box 130
Kure Beach, NC 28449

North West Seaport
P.O. Box 2865
Seattle, WA 98111

North Wind Undersea Institute
610 City Island Avenue
Bronx, NY 10464

Northport Historical Society
215 Main Street
Box 545
Northport, NY 11768

Northwest Michigan Maritime
  Museum
324 Main Street
P.O. Box 389
Frankfort, MI 49635

Old Lighthouse Museum
P.O. Box 512
Michigan City, IN 46360

Old Lighthouse Museum, Stonington
  Historical Society
P.O. Box 103
Stonington, CT 06378

Old Presque Isle Lighthouse Museum
6282 Blackbass Bay
Alpena, MI 49707

Oregon Historical Society
1230 SW Park Avenue
Portland, OR 97205

Oshkosh Public Museum
1331 Algoma Boulevard
Oshkosh, WI 54901

Oxford Maritime Museum
P.O. Box 178
Oxford, MD 21654

Oysterponds Historical Society
Village Lane
Orient, NY 11957

Pacific Fleet Submarine Memorial
  Association, Inc.
11 Arizona Memorial Drive
Honolulu, HI 96818

Paterson Museum
2 Market Place
Paterson, NJ 07501

Patriots Point Naval and Maritime
  Museum
P.O. Box 986
Mt. Pleasant, SC 29464

Penobscot Marine Museum
Lincoln Colcord Memorial Library
Church Street
Searsport, ME 04974

Philadelphia Ship Preservation Guild
Port of History Museum
Delaware & Spruce Streets
Philadelphia, PA 19106

Pittsburgh Historical Society
P.O. Box 1816
Pittsburgh, CA 94565

Plymouth Plantation, Inc.
P.O. Box 1620
Plymouth, MA 02360

Port Isabel Lighthouse State Historic
   Structure
P.O. Box 863
Port Isabel, TX 78578

Portsmouth Lightship Museum
London Slip at Water Street
P.O. Box 850
Portsmouth, VA 23704

Preservationists, Inc.
57 Concord Avenue
Leonardo, NJ 07737

Radcliffe Maritime Museum
Maryland Historical Society
201 West Monument Street
Baltimore, MD 21201

Ross County Historical Society, Inc.
45 West Fifth Street
Chillicothe, OH 45601

Sag Harbor Whaling and Historical
   Museum
P.O. Box 1327
Sag Harbor, NY 11963

San Diego Maritime Museum
1306 North Harbor Drive
San Diego, CA 92101

Sandy Bay Historical Society and
   Museum, Inc.
Box 179
Rockport, MA 01966

Sandy Hook Museum
Gateway National Recreation Area
P.O. Box 437
Highlands, NJ 07732

Sanilac Historical Museum
228 South Ridge Street
Port Sanilac, MI 48469

Shelburne Museum, Inc.
Shelburne, VT 05482

Ships of the Sea Maritime Museum
503 East River Street
Savannah, GA 31401

Shore Village Museum
104 Limerock Street
Rockland, ME 04841

Skenesborough Museum
Comstock Road
Whitehall, NY 12887

Sleeping Bear Dunes Seashore,
   National Park Service
400 Main Street
Frankfort, MI 49635

Smithsonian Institution
Museum of American History
12th & Constitution
Washington, DC 20560

Southampton Historical Museum
P.O. Box 303
Southampton, NY 11968

Southold Historical Society and
   Marine Museum
Main Road and Maple Lane
Southold, NY 11971

St. Clement's Island, Potomac
   Museum
General Delivery
Colton Point, MD 20626

St. Mary's City Commission
P.O. Box 39
St. Mary's City, MD 20686

Staten Island Historical Society
441 Clark Avenue
Staten Island, NY 10306

Staten Island Ferry Maritime Museum
New York Dept. of Maritime
St. George Ferry Term
Staten Island, NY 10314

Strawberry Banke, Inc.
P.O. Box 300
Portsmouth, NH 03801

Submarine Memorial Museum, USS
   Ling
P.O. Box 395
Hackensack, NJ 07602

Suffolk County Historical Society
300 West Main Street
Riverhead, NY 11901

Suffolk Marine Museum
Montauk Highway
P.O. Box 144
West Sayville, NY 11796

Susquehanna Museum of Havre de
   Grace, Inc.
P.O. Box 253
Havre de Grace, MD 21078

SS *Clipper* Foundation
600 East Grand Avenue
Navy Pier
Chicago, IL 60611

Tacoma Fireboat Museum Foundation
Nine St. Helens
Tacoma, WA 98402

Teysen's Talking Bear Museum
416 South Huron Avenue
Mackinaw City, MI 49701

U.S. Department of the Navy
Naval Historical Center, Bldg. 57
Washington Naval Yard
Washineton, DC 20374

U.S. Naval Academy Museum
Annapolis, MD 21402

USS *Alabama* Battleship Memorial
   Park
P.O. Box 65
Mobile, AL 36601

USS *Constitution* Museum
Building 22
Charlestown Navy Yard
Boston, MA 02129

USS *Massachusetts* Memorial
   Committee
Battleship Cove
Fall River, MA 02721

Vanderbilt Museum, Eagle's Nest
180 Little Neck Road
Centerport, NY 11721

Virginia Beach Historical Museum
P.O. Box 24
Virginia Beach, VA 23458

Wethersfield Historical Society
Old Academy Museum Library
150 Main Street
Wethersfield, CT 06103

Whale Museum
P.O. Box 945
Friday Harbor, WA 98250

Whaling Museum
P.O. Box 25
Cold Spring Harbor, NY 11724

Whatcom Museum of History and Art
121 Prospect Street
Bellingham, WA 98225

The H. Lee White Marine Museum
Foot of E First Street
P.O. Box 387
Oswego, NY 13126

White Pine Village, Hawley Museum
6187 S Lakeshore Drive
Ludington, MI 48431

Will County Historical Society
803 South State
St. Lockport, IL 60441

Willowbrook at Newfield
P.O. Box 80
Main Street
Newfield, ME 04056

Winona County Historical Museum
160 Johnson Street
Winona, MN 55987

The Henry Francis du Pont
   Winterthur Museum, Inc.
Winterthur, DE 19735

Index